Computer-Assisted Reporting

This straightforward how-to guide provides the basics of data analysis for news stories, effectively covering the tools and skills that any journalist or journalism student will need to master for reporting today. Brant Houston stresses the importance of accuracy and accountability in computer-assisted reporting, and alerts students to the potential and the pitfalls of utilizing large data sets in journalism.

Brant Houston, a professor and the Knight Chair in Investigative Reporting at the University of Illinois, is an international leader and innovator in investigative journalism. He served as the executive director of Investigative Reporters and Editors for more than a decade, is the current editor of *The Reporter's Handbook of Investigative Reporting*, and has conducted over 300 journalism seminars in twenty-five countries.

Computer-
Assisted
Reporting

A Pratical Guide

Fourth Edition

Brant Houston

Routledge
Taylor & Francis Group
NEW YORK AND LONDON

First published 2015
by Routledge
711 Third Avenue, New York, NY 10017

and by Routledge
2 Park Square, Milton Park, Abingdon, Oxon, OX14 4RN

Routledge is an imprint of the Taylor & Francis Group, an informa business

Library of Congress Cataloging in Publication Data
Houston, Brant.
  Computer-assisted reporting: a practical guide / by Brant Houston. —Fourth edition.
    pages cm
Includes bibliographical references and index.
1. Computer-assisted reporting. I. Title.
PN4784.E5H68 2014
070.40285—dc23

ISBN: 978-1-138-85503-8 (hbk)
ISBN: 978-0-7656-4219-6 (pbk)
ISBN: 978-1-315-72059-3 (ebk)

SUSTAINABLE
FORESTRY
INITIATIVE

Certified Sourcing
www.sfiprogram.org
SFI-00555

The SFI label applies to the text stock.

Printed and bound in the United States of America by
Walsworth Publishing Company, Marceline, MO.

Contents

Preface

It has been nearly three decades since I began using databases in my reporting, two decades since I began writing the first edition of this book, and a full decade since I completed the previous edition.

During those thirty years, software and hardware have constantly changed and evolved and, over time, have become much simpler to use. Heavy data analysis can be done on a laptop or desktop, online, or in the Cloud. Results can be visualized and shared across the Internet.

Meanwhile, the number of journalists using digital techniques and data has risen dramatically. A new generation of programmers and coders has joined newsrooms and journalists in analyzing data, bringing with them a fresh viewpoint and the skills to better visualize data and make it interactive.

Yet the need for a guide to help those just beginning to use databases for reporting purposes has not lessened. If anything, the demand has increased, as working journalists and journalism students realize the importance of obtaining the basic skills and the knowledge to use databases to create meaningful news stories through accurate analysis.

In journalism, finding interesting data, visualizing it, and presenting it in a pleasing format is not enough. Today's news audience wants to know what the data reveals and means and what analysis of the data says about whether systems and policies are working and society is being served. Many readers, viewers, and listeners seldom have the time to do their own data analysis or to follow through with the interviews and street work that must go along with such analysis.

Thus the purpose of this textbook remains the same as when I first wrote it: to provide a practical guide that is not based on a fascination with data or programming but instead focuses on coupling analysis with traditional reporting to produce more in-depth, more profound, and more useful journalism.

This book also is a product of my teaching the basics of computer-assisted reporting (CAR) in hundreds of seminars and conferences around the world. The evolution of this text also continues to benefit from listening to suggestions from students, teachers, journalists, and other readers. The result is a blending of a step-by-step approach to using software—an approach that never forgets the data, software, and analysis are all being implemented for better journalism.

The fourth edition of *Computer-Assisted Reporting* still provides students with advice on the data collection and analysis skills they need for news stories. The basics of CAR—finding and using data on the Internet, employing spreadsheets and/or database managers to analyze data, building your own databases, cleaning dirty data, and beginning to visualize the data—can help any journalist or student working with data achieve greater speed and insight. The basics can also help journalists and students discover, substantiate, and write successful stories on subjects they had not imagined before.

This helpful guide also addresses and stresses the need for accuracy in data analysis. While crowdsourcing during reporting or after publication has proven extremely helpful, initially publishing an authoritative story online with significant errors and then correcting through crowdsourcing does not really work. From the start, a journalist needs to keep errors to a minimum. Otherwise, journalism becomes just another voice of unverified information that lacks credibility or authority—and makes a journalist vulnerable to a lawsuit.

For the classroom or seminar, *Computer-Assisted Reporting* can be used as a core text or a supplement to any introductory or intermediate journalism textbook. Enhancing this edition also is valuable supplementary material on the Web.

Features

Because CAR is only as good as the stories it produces, this fourth edition includes reporting and writing advice for using CAR skills in daily and beat reporting. Other key features of *Computer-Assisted Reporting* have been retained and updated as needed:

- A practical approach that helps students master the basics, teaching them essential skills they need in concise, accessible language.
- Screenshots from software commonly used in journalism, such as Microsoft Excel and Access, and Google tools, that let students match what they see in the book to what they see on their screens and confirm their results.
- Real-life examples of news stories using CAR techniques, including both classics and new hits.
- "Your Turn to Practice" exercises that provide realistic and engaging assignments that give students the chance to practice the skills they have learned.
- Professional appendixes briefly introducing more advanced CAR skills, such as data mapping and social network analysis.

New to This Edition

To keep pace with the changing journalistic practices and help students clearly see how to apply CAR skills, material in this fourth edition will be linked with resources at Investigative Reporters and Editors (IRE) and the National Institute for Computer-Assisted Reporting (NICAR) to provide more exercises and tutorials online.

Other changes include:

- Exercises in spreadsheets and database managers that use more recent versions of Microsoft products.
- An updated chapter on researching, using, and downloading data found online.
- An emphasis on checking the integrity of data and publishing and presenting the results of data analysis in a way that does not require corrections or further explanation.
- Special online exercises and data relevant to international journalists.

Acknowledgments

I thank IRE and NICAR for their continued support for CAR and for the conference held each year that keeps professionals, professors, and students up to date with ever-changing technology and techniques. In particular, my thanks go out to Mark Horvit, the executive director of IRE and NICAR; longtime colleague in CAR Nils Mulvad; and former and current NICAR trainers Sarah Cohen, David Donald, Jaimi Dowdell, David Herzog, Jennifer LaFleur, Megan Luther, Jo Craven McGinty, Tom McGinty, Richard Mullins, Ron Nixon, Aron Pilhofer, Jeff Porter, and Neil Reisner.

I also appreciate the help provided by my former students—now accomplished journalists—in the development of previous editions. Those students include Jack Dolan, Justin Mayo, and John Sullivan. Foremost, I acknowledge the guidance and work of my mentors and pioneers in using data for journalism—Steve Doig, Elliot Jaspin, Philip Meyer, and Dwight Morris.

My thanks also go to my editor Suzanne Phelps Chambers, who oversaw the publication of the first edition. She encouraged me to do this fourth edition and has patiently overseen its development and publication. In addition, the close editing by Laura Brengelman has immensely helped in tightening and clarifying the writing and presentation.

Finally, my deepest thanks go to my wife, Rhonda Fallon, and to my parents, Joe and Liz Houston. They have always given their full support for my work in journalism, and that support has made all the difference.

One last word: Despite the expanding power and breadth of CAR, it remains only a tool for journalists. It aids, but does not replace, the imagination, experience, interviewing skills, intuition, skepticism, fieldwork, and passion of the dedicated journalist, whom I acknowledge last but not least.

Computer-Assisted Reporting

Data Journalism

What Computer-Assisted Reporting Is and Why Journalists Use It

It is in computer-assisted reporting where the real revolution is taking place, not only on the big analytical projects, but also in nuts-and-bolts newsgathering. New tools and techniques have made it possible for journalists to dig up vital information on deadline, to quickly add depth and context.

— Joel Simon and Carol Napolitano, "We're All Nerds Now," *The Columbia Journalism Review* (1999)

CAR gives journalists the opportunity to dig for truth in data, and the comparative analysis that a computer can do often reveals pertinent questions. What reporters are able to learn from using CAR provides readers with knowledge and insights that can cut through the clutter of opinionated noise and celebrity obsession. It also can allow even relatively small news operations to delve into problems affecting the global community, yet speak to readers and viewers right around the block.

— Jason Method, "The Benefits of Computer-Assisted Reporting," *Nieman Reports* (2008)

The words in the first quote were written as the twentieth century was coming to an end, but they remain true as we move deeper into the twenty-first century. The words in the second quote, nearly a decade later, show how crucial computer-assisted reporting has become in creating credibility and in recognizing the globalization of news.

But there is still a revolution going on in journalism when it comes to data, both at basic and extraordinarily high levels.

In the past decade, software for analysis has continued to become much simpler to use. An overwhelming amount of data is now online and easy to download. Storage space is immense on hard drives, flash drives, and in the Cloud. The computing power on a laptop, tablet, or mobile phone dwarfs the power available only a few years ago. The ability to visualize data for better understanding and analysis has become pro forma. Furthermore, a new generation of computer programmers has joined traditional journalists to tackle the problems of capturing data from the Web, cleaning and organizing it, and creating fascinating presentations to be shared with the public and to encourage citizen participation and analysis.

At the same time, many fundamental truths remain the same. Databases are still created by people, and thus they naturally have omissions and errors that people have made and that must be noted and corrected. Every database also is a slice in time and thus is outdated the moment it is acquired and used.

Also remember that a database alone is not a story. Instead, it is a field of information that needs to be harvested carefully with insight and caution. It needs to be compared with and augmented with observation and interviews.

More important than ever is determining the accuracy of a database before using it. Equally important is careful analysis of the data, since one small error can result in monstrously wrong conclusions. The idea of uploading data on the Web and hoping the public or volunteers will consistently make sense of it with reliable analysis has proven unreliable. In fact, journalists—not advocates—are needed more than ever to deliver a well-researched understanding of information and data, and to tell a compelling story using data. Yet, despite changes in technology and the availability of mega-data, some scenarios have not changed.

For example, as a local reporter in the United States, you may want to look into how many inmates are in state jails because they cannot come up with the money for bail so they can be free until trial. You see that a recent audit of jails points out that many persons are in jail not because they have been convicted, but because they simply don't have the finances to pay the bail set for them. Furthermore, it appears anecdotally that judges are setting higher bails for black and Hispanic males than white males. With a little research, you find that the county jails keep records on inmates that include the amount of bail in each case and each inmate's race and gender. After a series of meetings, the officials agree to give you the database with the information you need. They don't want to put it online for you to retrieve, but they will give you a DVD containing the database.

By the next morning, you do your first analysis of the data and see that the bail for black and Hispanic males is usually double that for whites, even when they are charged with the same crime and have the same criminal and personal background. Over the next few weeks, you check through the records and gather more details. You recheck your information, look at other documents, conduct interviews, and write the story. The work culminates in a front-page story that presents a systematic look at justice gone wrong. The best answer the officials have is the system discriminates against the poor, not just blacks and Hispanics.

Or consider this more recent scenario: You want to know how weak security is at your nearby metropolitan airport. So you get local police reports or download recent information from the Transportation Security Administration. You begin by analyzing the database, which consists of counting the number of violations at your local airport in recent years, and then closely examine the details of those violations.

You quickly find serious and surprising violations in which guns, knives, and other weapons are seized. You follow up with research on the Web and interviews with airport officials, law enforcement, and airline companies. You review reports by government investigators posted on the Web. Within days, you have an important story that the public needs to know.

In fact, more than 100 news organizations used local police databases while doing airport security stories in the weeks following the terrorists' attacks in the United States on September 11, 2001. More recently, journalism students at Medill wrote this very story and created an online database to go with it.

As you will learn in this book, the techniques described in these scenarios are known as *computer-assisted reporting*, also referred to as CAR, and they are a part of everyday journalism. Journalists use these and other techniques for daily reporting, reporting on the beat, and for the large projects that win Pulitzer Prizes. In the past decade, journalism awards have gone to *The Washington Post* for stories on police shootings and child abuse; to *The Sun Sentinel*, of Fort Lauderdale, Florida, which used transponder toll records to investigate reckless speeding by off-duty police officers; and to the small newspaper the *Bristol Herald Courier* in Virginia for the work of reporter Daniel Gilbert, who built and used a database as part of his investigation into natural-gas royalties owed to thousands of landowners in southwest Virginia.

Computer-assisted reporting does not refer to journalists sitting at a keyboard writing stories or surfing the Web. It refers to downloading databases and doing data analysis that can provide context and depth to daily stories. It refers to techniques of producing tips that launch more complex stories from a broader perspective and with a better understanding of the issues. A journalist beginning a story with the knowledge of the patterns gleaned from 150,000 court records is way ahead of a reporter who sees only a handful of court cases each week.

Computer-assisted reporting doesn't replace proven journalistic practices. It has become a part of them. It also requires greater responsibility and vigilance. The old standard—"verify, verify, verify"— that one learns in basic reporting classes becomes ever more critical. "Healthy skepticism" becomes ever more important. The idea of interviewing multiple sources and cross-referencing them becomes ever more crucial.

"Computers don't make a bad reporter into a good reporter. What they do is make a good reporter better," Elliot Jaspin, one of the pioneers in computer-assisted reporting, warned three decades ago. Many practicing journalists have sought training in the past two decades and become proficient in the basic skills of computer-assisted reporting. They have overcome computer and math phobia, and they now put these skills to use on a daily basis. And this has led to more precision and sophistication in their reporting.

To quote Philip Meyer, a pioneer in database analysis for news stories, "They are raising the ante on what it takes to be journalist." Aiding in the progress and acceptance of these skills has been the proliferation of the Web and social media, the development of inexpensive and easy-to-use computers and software, and the increased attention to the value of data and techniques of analysis in newsrooms.

Computer-assisted reporting is no longer a sidebar to mainstream journalism. It is essential to surviving as a journalist in the twenty-first century. The tools of computer-assisted reporting won't replace a good journalist's imagination, ability to conduct revealing interviews, or talent to develop sources. But a journalist who knows how to use computers in day-to-day and long-term work will gather and analyze information more quickly, and develop and deliver a deeper understanding. The journalist will be better prepared for interviews and be able to write with more authority. That journalist also will see potential stories that would have never occurred to him or her.

The journalist also will achieve parity with politicians, bureaucrats, and businessmen who have enjoyed many advantages over the journalists simply because they had the money and knowledge to utilize databases and digital information before journalists did. Government officials and workers have long been comfortable entering information into computers and then retrieving and analyzing it. Businesses, small and large, routinely use spreadsheet and database software. Advocacy groups frequently employ databases to push their agendas.

Without a rudimentary knowledge of the advantages and disadvantages of data analysis, it is difficult for the contemporary journalist to understand and report on how the world now works. And it is far more difficult for a journalist to do meaningful public service journalism or to perform the necessary watchdog role.

As long ago as 1990, Frank Daniels III, executive editor of *The News & Observer* in Raleigh, North Carolina, recognized the challenge. He began his newspaper's early and oft-lauded push into computer-assisted reporting because the 1990 campaign of then Senator Jesse Helms was profoundly more computer-sophisticated than Daniels's own newspaper. "It made me realize how stupid we were, and I don't like feeling stupid," Daniels recalled.

Daniels was right about the bad position in which journalists had put themselves. For years, journalists were like animals in a zoo, waiting to be fed pellets of information by the keepers who are happy for journalists to stay in their Luddite cages. But a good journalist always wants to see original information, because every time other people select or sort that information, they can add "spin" or bias, which can be tough to detect. Computer-assisted reporting can help prevent that from happening.

Many journalists and journalism students now learn the basic tools of computer-assisted reporting because they realize that it is the best way to get to the information since most governmental and commercial records are now stored electronically. Despite security concerns, there still are a mind-boggling number of databases on U.S. government and international Websites. So without the ability to deal with electronic data, a journalist is cut off from some of the best and untainted information. The old-fashioned journalist will never get to the information on time—or worse, will be brutally trampled by the competing media.

For a journalist or journalism student, this knowledge also is crucial in the competition to getting a good job. At many news organizations, an applicant who has these skills—which are far more than the ability to surf the Web—gets his or her résumé moved to the top of the stack.

A journalist does not have to be a programmer or someone who knows software code, although that also can make a huge difference. A journalist who can use a spreadsheet or database manager is free to thoroughly explore information, reexamine it, and reconsider what it means in relation to interviews and observations in the field. The journalist can take the spin off the information and get closer to the truth. A journalist may not be a statistician, but a good journalist knows enough about statistics to know how easy it is to manipulate them or lie with them. In the same way, if a journalist understands how data can be manipulated, he or she can better judge a bureaucrat's spin on the facts or a government's misuse of a database.

Journalists have found, too, that if they let a person whose job is only to process data do the analysis, nuances or potential pitfalls of the data may be missed. A data programmer also does not necessarily think like a journalist; what may be significant for the journalist may seem unimportant to the programmer. Using a data programmer to do all the work is like asking someone else to read a book for you.

The conscientious journalist also does not want to fall into a cycle of asking for a report in some frozen digital format, studying the report, coming up with more questions, and then asking for another report. Why get into a lengthy back-and-forth when you can engage in a rapid, multidimensional conversation with the data on your computer screen?

Most important, computer-assisted reporting is at the heart of public service journalism and of vigilant daily reporting. This is true whether writing about education, business, government, environmental issues, or any other topic.

History of Computer-Assisted Reporting

Many practitioners date the beginning of computer-assisted reporting to 1952, when CBS tried to use experts with a mainframe computer to predict the outcome of the presidential election. That's a bit of a stretch, or perhaps it was a false beginning because it wasn't until 1967 that data analysis started to catch on.

In that year, Philip Meyer at *The Detroit Free Press* in Michigan used a mainframe to analyze a survey of Detroit residents for the purpose of understanding and explaining the serious riots that erupted in the city that summer. Meyer went on to work in the 1970s with *The Philadelphia Inquirer* reporters Donald Barlett and James Steele to analyze the sentencing patterns in the local court system and with Rich Morin at *The Miami Herald* in Florida to analyze property assessment records. He also wrote a book called *Precision Journalism* that explained and advocated using database analysis and social research methods in reporting. (Several revisions of the book have been published since then.)

Still, only a few journalists used these techniques until the mid-1980s, when Elliot Jaspin received recognition, while at *The Providence-Journal Bulletin* in Rhode Island, for analyzing databases for stories, including those on dangerous school bus drivers and on a political scandal involving home loans. At the same time, other journalists across the country, often consulting with Meyer or Jaspin, began doing data analysis for their stories.

Aiding their efforts were improved personal computers and a program—Nine Track Express—that Jaspin and journalist-programmer Daniel Woods wrote to make it easier to transfer computer tapes (which contain nine "tracks" of information) to personal computers using a portable tape drive. This allowed journalists to circumvent the bureaucracies and delays involved in using mainframes.

In 1989, the profession recognized the value of computer-assisted reporting when it gave a Pulitzer Prize to *The Atlanta Journal-Constitution* in Georgia for its stories on racial disparities in home loan practices. During the same year, Jaspin established the institute at the Missouri School of Journalism now known as the National Institute for Computer-Assisted Reporting (NICAR), and in 1990 Indiana University professor James Brown held the first computer-assisted reporting conference in Indianapolis. Since that time, use of computer-assisted reporting has blossomed, primarily due to the seminars conducted throughout the world by NICAR and Investigative Reporters and Editors (IRE) as part of a joint program. The Global Investigative Journalism Network also has worked with IRE on training worldwide.

Since 2001, the use of computer-assisted reporting—often referred to as data journalism—has spread throughout the world. Data analysis for news stories is being done routinely in Europe, Latin America, Asia, Africa, and Australia. There are now international awards for the use of data for news stories, particularly for visualization of data. Much of this advance in international data analysis has been spurred by training by IRE and NICAR, as well as the Global Investigative Journalism Network, which holds conferences every two years with a heavy emphasis on computer-assisted reporting.

The Basic Tools

Over time, three skills (which are the focus of this book) for computer-assisted reporting have emerged: online resources (primarily finding and downloading databases), spreadsheets, and database managers. As journalists have become more technologically sophisticated, other tools have joined these three, including statistical software, geographical information systems (GIS), or *mapping software*, and social network analysis.

Since then, journalists have added such techniques as Web scraping (automatically downloading individual records from the Web and collating them into a database) and new methods of cleaning and presenting data through programming languages such as Python. But in providing training to thousands of journalists since 1989, IRE and NICAR have found that the beginning journalist in computer-assisted reporting starts most comfortably with the first three tools.

Online resources are available to journalists through a variety of ways. Online resources include (1) e-mail, (2) discussion groups, (3) social media, and (4) active and archived databases, where records are stored. With online resources you can look up court records, retrieve campaign records or the national census of countries, and find thousands of other databases.

Spreadsheet software such as Microsoft Excel is good for analyzing numbers. You should think about using a spreadsheet whenever you are looking at salaries, budgets, census data, prices, or statistical reports. A spreadsheet allows you to quickly filter and sum columns of numbers, compare them, sort them, and put your results into charts. While a spreadsheet can allow you to do much more, these are routine uses for basic computer-assisted reporting.

A *database manager* such as Microsoft Access is good for searching, summarizing, and relating different files known as tables. A database manager can group similar kinds of information and link different files through keywords or identification numbers. It enables you to look up information about a person quickly by name, street address, or phone number. It enables you to look up political contributions to a particular candidate, group those contributions, and total them. It enables you to match the names in one file of information, such as death certificates, to names in another file, such as voters. (There's always a potential story when you find dead people voting.)

A database manager also can deftly handle many more records than a spreadsheet, especially when you have several files. The more advanced tools of computer-assisted reporting are:

Statistical software becomes attractive later when a journalist feels more comfortable with numbers and wants to perform more detailed and robust analysis. (SPSS or SAS are two common brands, and R, also called GNU S, is a popular open-source software.) Journalists use it for looking at such topics as school testing scores or racial disparities in mortgages or insurance.

GIS or *mapping software* (one of the simplest being Google Fusion Tables and the more common and sophisticated for government data being ArcView, distributed by the company Esri) helps illustrate the points made in a story and illuminates disclosures that otherwise would remain unseen. Journalists often use it for election votes, dangerous environmental areas, and many other topics. One famous landmark use involved the red and blue election map by *USA Today* in the year 2000. The newspaper color-coded states depending on which presidential candidate—Bush or Gore—the state voted for. Comedians even used the map for jokes on the election.

Social networking software (ranging from a plug-in to Microsoft Excel called NodeXL to many free open-source programs) visually draws connections between people and/or organizations. Journalists are beginning to more frequently use this software; one group started a Website called Muckety.com intended to help other journalists diagram these networks. Anthropologists, business consultants, intelligence and police agencies, and health researchers have already used this kind of software and analysis to explore and expose relationships.

This book will concentrate on the basic tools and analysis that can get you going in a classroom or newsroom. This book will strip away the distractions (like computer manuals) that seem so plentiful when you begin learning how to use software, and it will show you shortcuts to doing effective stories. The book also will put the use of software into the context of journalism and day-to-day reporting.

Trial and Error, and Repetition

The best way to learn computer-assisted reporting is through trial and error. *You have to practice.* You have to make mistakes in asking questions of the information. You need to try different queries in database managers, look at the result, and try again to see if you can better focus your inquiry and the answers to it. You need to be intellectually daring and creative to think of the variables that could affect a conclusion.

The exercises that accompany this book can be found on the Web at www.ire.org/carbook/. They will give you plenty of opportunities to try different ways of arranging data and to discover the best way to find valid answers. Moreover, you have to realize that despite all the software advances, computer software still has quirks, multiple icons, and obscure keystrokes. Practice is the way to become more comfortable with the tools.

Where You're Going

Part 1 of this book, "Learning Computer-Assisted Reporting Skills," concentrates on the basic skills. Part 2, "Using Computer-Assisted Reporting in News Stories," focuses on producing computer-assisted stories and overcoming common newsgathering problems that occur when you use these skills.

The first section concentrates on learning the basic computer-assisted reporting skills for sorting, filtering, and summarizing data. These skills include downloading data from Websites and importing it into spreadsheets and database managers; using math, charts, and other tools in spreadsheets to analyze data; and using database managers to search, summarize, and compare databases.

The second section focuses on doing stories with computer-assisted reporting. It covers dealing with the practical challenges of finding and negotiating for data, cleaning up dirty data, building a database when there isn't one, and weaving it all together to produce better news stories.

In Part 1, Chapter 2 offers tips for searches on the Web for data sets, the use of e-mail discussion groups, and downloading data. In recent years, many public databases have been uploaded to the Web; this means a journalist doing computer-assisted reporting can get useful data without having to go through the often-painful process of requesting it from officials. This chapter points to some of the most common Websites and indexes from which to obtain data. It also discusses the columns and rows format of a data table, the challenges with downloading the data, and judging the accuracy of data.

Once a journalist has downloaded data to the computer, he or she is able to do some basic analysis and browsing. Chapter 3 introduces spreadsheets, which most journalists agree is the fundamental tool for starting out in computer-assisted analysis. Spreadsheets also are a good way for a journalist to get comfortable with basic math, and many of the examples look at how math is applied to cut through the spin that politicians or bureaucrats put on numbers.

Chapter 4 deals with the more advanced uses of spreadsheets that filter, reshape, visualize, and interpret data. This chapter introduces the idea of grouping records and counting them. The chapter also shows some basic charts and graphs that a spreadsheet can produce to make numbers more understandable. This chapter serves as a bridge to the next chapter on database managers by discussing the similarities of data analysis in spreadsheets and database managers.

Chapter 5 describes the basics of database managers, which can be a bit more difficult to learn but are the logical next step in data analysis after using spreadsheets. Database managers are frequently used for grouping categories of records and for linking one file of information to another. They do these tasks much more powerfully than a spreadsheet and handle many more records than a spreadsheet.

Database managers allow you quickly to select columns of information, filter in or filter out certain kinds of information, group some items together, and then order the results. In addition, you may link one file of information in a database to another, or do what is sometimes called matchmaking. Chapter 5 focuses on learning searching and grouping techniques. This chapter uses the "query by example" interface provided by the software Microsoft Access.

Chapter 6 continues with the application of database managers for journalism and shows how to link files. This chapter uses Structured Query Language, better known as SQL. While SQL might seem a bit intimidating, it often is a more rapid and intuitive way of examining data for stories. If a journalist knows SQL, the journalist quickly can learn and use any database manager, which is helpful as software rapidly evolves.

Part 2 deals with pursuing a news story and the challenges a journalist faces in doing so. Chapter 7 discusses strategy for getting data that officials are reluctant to distribute, but that may be much more detailed and richer with useful information. Laws that have only begun to catch up with technology and concerns over security and privacy pose barriers to obtaining databases. This chapter examines some of the common obstacles presented by bureaucrats and commercial vendors and advises you on how to get around them. The chapter also looks at methods for finding the right database for the story, requesting the data, and negotiating for data at a reasonable price and within a reasonable time.

Chapter 8 gives you the steps for creating your own databases when a government won't release them or when they don't exist. This chapter is intended to help especially journalists and student journalists in small communities in the United States and other countries whose governments or campuses do not make databases available or do not collect information electronically.

Chapter 9 discusses "dirty data." Dirty data consists of incomplete or incorrect databases that need to be "cleaned," that is, completed or corrected. Most, if not all, databases contain errors (just like news reports). A journalist needs to know how to find those errors and either correct them or note them. The cleaning up of dirty data can become complex, but Chapter 9 touches on some of the basic concepts and methods.

In Chapter 10, we talk about strategies for finding and getting started on computer-assisted stories and how *not* to get lost in the abundance of information and possibilities. We look at the steps in doing computer-assisted reporting and how to effectively write a story that uses computer-assisted reporting techniques; review examples and methods to ensure that numbers don't overwhelm a story; and verify that the anecdotal material is representative of the trends and facts discovered while doing data analysis. The chapter also contains advice for how editors and news directors can manage and supervise computer-assisted reporting.

The appendixes to this book are aimed at students and professional, practicing journalists taking the next step after the basics. Both groups need to be aware of the more advanced tools. Among the topics covered are GIS (or mapping software), social networking software, and choosing equipment and software.

Practical Advice

Computer-assisted reporting is always an adventure with a multitude of possibilities and outcomes. This handbook does not attempt to cover everything; instead, it offers enough practical advice to jump-start the hesitant student or journalist into using it for daily, beat, or long-term reporting. One final thought before we get started: a journalist's success in learning computer-assisted reporting depends on that journalist's own efforts—no matter how difficult or frustrating it may be, or how much computer-assisted reporting may drive you crazy. But in any event, you need it to be a journalist in the twenty-first century. It's like the old vaudeville joke:

> *A man goes to a doctor and says, "My brother is making me crazy."*
> *The doctor asks why, and the man says, "Because my brother thinks he's a chicken."*
> *The doctor says, "Well, tell him he's not a chicken."*
> *"But Doc," says the man, "I need the eggs."*

Face it. You need the eggs.

CAR Wars

> *Analyzing city employee salaries for a story on pay equity was reinforced by three lessons I learned at the NICAR boot camp:*
>
> - *Do your homework.*
> - *Get everything.*
> - *Guarantee a "minimum" story.*
>
> *When I approached the personnel directors in cities in the Salt Lake area, I was told that I could have a range of salaries but not the exact earnings of employees. However, I knew from researching my state's open records laws that salaries had to be disclosed. I learned the hard way about getting everything. I had only asked for employee names, salaries, and job tables. I soon realized I also needed information on tenure and the city department in which an employee worked. I ended up going back to the cities. I also had neglected to push for record layouts*

and code sheets. In this case, I was able to work through the problems.

Third, I learned the value of "the minimum story." The most obvious thing—and the easiest story to do—was that female employees were very scarce in top management. I pursued that angle and found that women who get the same jobs as men earned comparable salaries, but the hang-up was that few women crossed the line from traditional female jobs to traditional male jobs, including top management.

—Edward Carter, *The Deseret News*, Utah

Chapter Checklist

- Journalists need to know how to search for and analyze information on computers because governments and businesses are using computers to store and distribute information. It also is a skill that is needed to compete with other news organizations or to get better jobs.
- The three primary tools of computer-assisted reporting are spread-sheets, database managers, and online resources for finding and downloading data.
- Once learned, computer-assisted reporting permits a journalist to quickly gather and analyze comprehensive information.
- The best ways to learn the basic software tools are through trial and error, repetition, and intellectually creativity.

Your Turn to Practice

1. Identify three news stories that used computer-assisted reporting to ana-lyze government databases and won Pulitzer Prizes. Find explanations on how those stories were done. Hint: Go the Website of Investigative Reporters and Editors, www.ire.org/resourcecenter, for each of these assignments, or the Pulitzer Prizes Website, www.pulitzer.org.
2. Identify three news stories that used computer-assisted reporting on breaking news stories and on follow-up stories. Find explanations on how those stories were done.
3. Find versions of database managers such as Microsoft Access and of spreadsheet software such as Microsoft Excel. Open each of these pro-grams and take a look at their basic appearances and tools.

Part 1

Learning Computer-Assisted Reporting Skills

Online Resources

Researching and Finding Data Online

> Newsday's *series revealed that doctors who have been punished for serious or even fatal wrongdoing often continue to work for managed health-care companies.*
>
> *The health-care companies and agencies probably never envisioned their Websites being scrutinized in the manner reporter Thomas Maier examined them. From the board-certification Website, he found doctors who erroneously claimed board certification in the Web listings of managed care companies.*
>
> —Richard J. Dalton Jr., *Newsday*

Maier's reporting, assisted by database expert Dalton, included the use of a huge database, numerous interviews, and a successful open-record lawsuit. But as noted, it was an early example of cross-referencing data on different Websites. The concept was straightforward: compare lists of doctors who had been disciplined with the list of doctors who were part of a managed care network.

Savvy journalists now routinely compare data on Websites and mine Websites for data with advanced searches that specifically look for government data. One effective search specifies that the domain name end in .gov and the file type be .xls, indicating that the file is a Microsoft Excel spreadsheet. **Figure 2.1** shows a search for government spreadsheets on poverty.

Figure 2.1

Overall, a journalist uses online information for several purposes, including:

- *Research.* A journalist can go to the Internet to find databases by searching through books, news stories, academic papers, government reports, and other documents.
- *Interviews.* Online reporting allows a journalist to widen the inquiry and get more information about a database by searching for people involved in or knowledgeable about the database, such as experts, victims, witnesses, and participants.
- *Database gathering.* A journalist can download data to his or her own computer, especially when the data comes in different files for

different time periods or when only one record or a small group of records can be accessed at a time.

- *Data analysis.* When journalists find a particular database that could be useful, they can use a spreadsheet or database manager on their own computers, or now, more frequently, they can access an analysis program on the server where the database is located.

In this chapter, we will take a quick look at useful online information and research techniques and then concentrate on finding databases and downloading them.

Finding Data

Before you use a database, you first have to find it. And the one you want to find is a database that is organized in columns and rows because that format is the easiest to analyze.

Reporters still do much of their basic analysis working with columns and rows of data, often in a Google or Microsoft Excel spreadsheet or in a database manager such as Microsoft Access. Columns and rows allow reporters to sort and summarize data easily in what Richard Mullins, a longtime computer-assisted reporting (CAR) practitioner, likes to call the "two-dimensional world"—that is, a world reduced to a flat screen of vertical and horizontal information.

In news reports and on news Websites, we find pages and pages of columns and rows, or tabular information. You may find charts of names and numbers in the front section about such things as census studies, budgets, and taxes. In the business pages, you will find pages of columns and rows detailing stocks, bonds, and mutual funds. In the sports pages, you constantly find the statistics of teams and athletes presented in tabular data form.

We ponder the two-dimensional world every day. If we are interested in sports, we check the standings of teams. The first column in **Figure 2.2** contains the team name, the second column gives the number of wins, and the third lists the losses.

As you can see in **Figure 2.2**, the columns are categories of information, and each row (also known as a *record*) has information for each category for a particular team. On paper and in the often-used, portable document format (PDF), columns and rows are "petrified" information. That is, the records are static and can't be easily sorted, filtered, or have calculations performed on them.

Figure 2.2

Team	Wins	Losses
Texas	6	3
Nebraska	5	4
Arkansas	4	5
Florida	3	6
Maryland	2	7

But import those records into a spreadsheet or a database manager, and it suddenly becomes easy to search and rearrange them in more meaningful ways. With basic software tools, you can change the order of the columns and rows, and you can group categories of data and total it or perform other calculations on it. You also can more readily compare it with other data.

For example, journalists frequently want to look at how much public employee salaries are costing taxpayers and who is getting the highest salary. The information regarding people's salaries has at least three categories: name, title, and salary. Each row is a record of each person's information. On paper, you have to clumsily rearrange it by hand. In a spreadsheet, you can quickly sort such a list.

Here, in **Figure 2.3**, we have salary information in a Word document:

Figure 2.3

Salaries		
Name	Title	Annual Salary
Josephine Smith	Comptroller	$54,000
Juan Hinojosa	City Manager	$72,000
James Brown	Purchasing Agent	$44,000
Joan Bertrand	Parks Director	$48,000

With the two basic tools of CAR—the spreadsheet and database manager—you could look at this kind of list and sort it. In **Figure 2.4**, we easily sorted salaries from high to low in a spreadsheet:

Figure 2.4

	A	B	C
1	Salaries		
2	Name	Title	Annual Salary
3	Juan Hinojosa	City Manager	$72,000
4	Josephine Smith	Comptroller	$54,000
5	Joan Bertrand	Parks Director	$48,000
6	James Brown	Purchasing Agent	$44,000

Whether there are four rows of names or 100,000 rows of names, it doesn't matter to a spreadsheet or a database manager when it comes to sorting. With the same command you can quickly sort from the highest at the top to the lowest at the bottom—or vice versa.

Digital Information and Data on the Internet

Before you can do any analysis, you first have to find and obtain the data. There are several basic ways to do this. You can download data from the Web, acquire it on a storage device such as a DVD or flash drive, or build a database yourself. (In this chapter, we will focus on getting data from the Web.)

With the explosion of information on the Web, finding the right data can be time-consuming and frustrating. But if you approach the Web with a plan and an understanding of what is possible to find, you will reap rich results.

Using Online Resources

Although some journalists still struggle with the practical use of online resources, most have learned to make use of them for daily stories and long-term projects.

As long ago as the early 1980s, reporters at *American Banker* and at *The Kansas City Star* in Missouri used LexisNexis (www.lexisnexis. com)—a fee-based service of news articles and lawsuits—to research background information and find court cases from across the nation to track international con men who caused the collapse of dozens of lending institutions. Using keywords for the con men and banks, the reporters identified which states' lending institutions were affected.

In 1991, Mike Berens, a journalist then at *The Columbus Dispatch* in Ohio, used an online news-clipping library to create a database that tracked a multistate serial killer. By selecting and reviewing unsolved murders of women along interstates, Berens recognized a pattern of killings.

Others have used online databases to detail the deaths of persons from radiation poisoning, measure pollution from environmental toxic sites, track increased housing development in landslide- and earthquake-prone areas, and track nonprofit organization spending. Online forums and social media have helped reporters gather information on terrorist bombings, mass shootings, and city riots.

What Online Resources to Use

One way to research better online is to think of it in two major forms, as suggested by the *Investigative Reporter's Handbook* (Brant Houston and IRE, 2009): (1) traditional secondary resources, such as the sometimes costly archives of newspapers, academic papers, and business and court records; and (2) primary resources, such as government databases, social media, and discussion groups that cost little or nothing.

The next challenge is to know whether you can trust what you find. Well, "trust" is probably not the right word. As said earlier, you have to verify and cross-reference whatever you find in the online world. You need to determine what Websites are credible and who created them. As noted earlier, Websites that have addresses ending in .gov are constructed by government agencies and consequently should be as reliable as any other government information. Others are run by nonprofit groups, some nonpartisan and some advocating for a cause. Still others are run by businesses or individuals, often using government databases.

As a good journalist, you need to accurately identify the source of the data, do interviews, and compare the information you find with data from other sources that support or contradict information in the database.

Digital Library Researchers and Journalists

Library researchers are one of the key resources for a journalist working online. Professional researchers know where information is stored and how to find it with the right tools. A professional researcher can serve as a guide, providing invaluable advice and knowledge, helping with complex searches, and pointing the journalist to the right resources.

A great example of such an adept researcher is Paul Myers, who works at the British Broadcasting Corporation in London. Myers freely shares his techniques at his Website, Research Clinic (http://researchclinic.net). Another notable researcher is Margot Williams, who has worked at *The Washington Post*, *The New York Times*, National Public Radio, and the Center for Public Integrity. Williams often shares her methods in tip sheets that she distributes at journalism conferences.

But journalists need to learn the basics of going into the digital stacks themselves to directly access the data they want and to ask better questions during their reporting. This is the same principle as learning to use spreadsheets and database managers instead of relying on someone else to do all of your data analysis.

Newsroom Databases

Digital collections of news articles can be extremely valuable in finding databases that have proven useful. There are several commercial services—such as LexisNexis or NewsBank (www.newsbank.com) that provide this kind of resource. Library researchers are skilled in the searching of newspaper archives, and a good journalist never starts a story without checking the archives. The service is often free for university faculty and students, but the charges can be significant for private individuals and newsrooms.

Discussion Groups and Social Media

Online discussion groups, such as various listservs or Google Groups, are also constant sources for finding good databases. Social media such as Twitter, Facebook, LinkedIn, Tumblr, and others have discussions about databases.

You can join discussion groups or forums in which journalists and programmers discuss data problems and issues. A further advantage of these discussion groups is that you can ask a question of hundreds or thousands of persons at one time. You also can search the archives of these discussion groups to see what has been said.

One long-running listserv to join if you are a journalist or journalism student is the listserv of the National Institute for Computer-Assisted Reporting (NICAR), as shown in an excerpted e-mail exchange in **Figure 2.5**.

Figure 2.5

> to NICAR-L
>
> Howdy folks!
>
> I'm posting this question from a colleague here so bear with me if you guys have many questions afterwards.
>
> I have hundreds of separate spreadsheets, each with two worksheets. The only worksheet that I'm interested in contains data under identical headings in the identical columns, but has various numbers of rows.
>
> Is there any program out there that would allow the merging of each worksheet from the hundreds of spreadsheets into one Excel spreadsheet or one Access table?
>
> Or do I have to copy and paste each worksheet from each spreadsheet into one spreadsheet and/or import each into Access and thus requiring hundreds of actions?

Let's say journalist Helen Jenks wants to join this listserv. She would send a message, as shown in **Figure 2.6**.

Figure 2.6

> To: listserv@lists.missouri.edu
>
> Subscribe NICAR-L Helen Jenks

As a result, she would be able to see messages in which people talk about how to do CAR. As shown in **Figure 2.5**, she also could send messages to the listserv asking for help or information.

Using Boolean Logic to Search the Internet

Journalists can waste a lot of time bouncing around the Web looking for databases and specific data subsets if they do not know enough about searching. We will cover Boolean logic in more detail in later chapters because it is the way to methodically search databases and create subsets of databases. But every journalist should know the power and impact of three Boolean words—*and*, *or*, and *not*—when used in searches.

For example, if you are looking for information on dogs *and* fleas, you will get only information that involves both. If you type that you are looking for information on dogs *or* fleas, you will get a great deal more information because your search results will include information just about dogs, just about fleas, and about both dogs and fleas. If you type that you are looking for information about dogs and *not* fleas, then you will get information about dogs not involving fleas.

Many search engines, such as Google.com or Bing.com, automatically choose whether to use *and* or *or* without guidance from you. So, as *The Wall Street Journal* investigative reporter and expert searcher Tom McGinty suggests, you should always read each search engine's tips. Here, in **Figure 2.7**, you can see the beginning of Google's search tips and tricks.

Figure 2.7

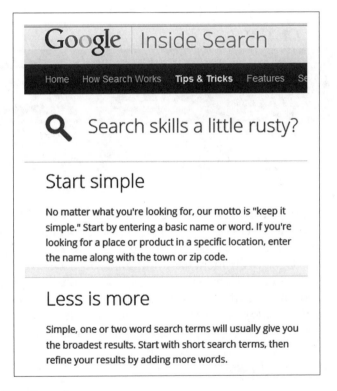

Downloading Databases

There are now ways to shortcut your searches by going to the portals that collate or index free government databases. These portals may access international, national, regional, or local databases. Both Yahoo.com and a Website called SearchSystems.net (www.searchsystems.net) also collect and categorize databases around the world.

In the United States, sites such as Data.gov (www.data.gov) offer thousands of U.S. government databases that can be downloaded or analyzed quickly with the methods of spreadsheets and database managers. You can also do some basic analysis with the tools on the site—such as filtering and mapping—before deciding whether to download the data. In fact, working with data on that site can be good tutorial in basic data analysis, as shown in **Figure 2.8**.

Figure 2.8

Many government agencies throughout the world also have sections of their Websites devoted to statistics and data such as the United Nations's data explorer site shown in **Figure 2.9**.

The U.S. government has additional gateways to data on both the U.S. and international sites; one example is the U.S. Census Bureau, which we will discuss later in this chapter. Of course, no online portal or index is necessarily complete, but the Census Bureau's Website (www.census.gov) is a valuable place to start.

Different File Types

Databases from the Web can come in many forms, most of which can be imported with relative ease into Microsoft Excel or Microsoft Access. For example, the U.S. Census Bureau offers files in several formats. (See **Figure 2.10**.)

Figure 2.9

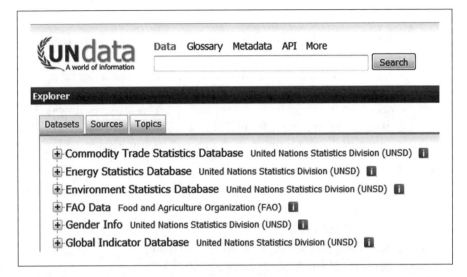

Figure 2.10

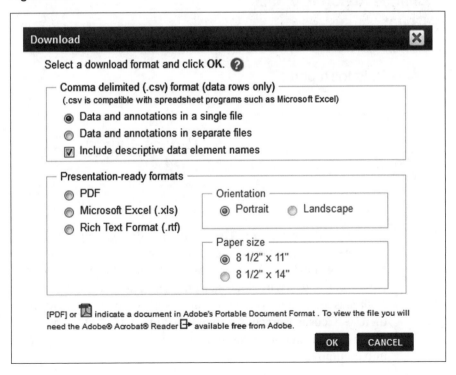

Here is a short list of the common file formats used for databases:

- *Excel or database files.* These files are often listed with .xls or .dbf as the file extension name, as shown before.
- *Hypertext Markup Language or HTML files.* These are tables that have extensions of .html or .php and that often can be read and opened automatically by a spreadsheet. You also can download a file or copy and paste it quickly into a spreadsheet such as the file on waiting lists for organ transplants shown in **Figure 2.11**.

Figure 2.11

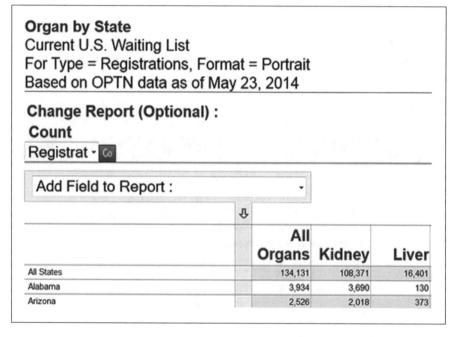

- *Text or fixed format files.* These have the data evenly lined up in straight columns; the file names often have the extension .txt. These files can be imported into a spreadsheet through its import "wizard." Or you can copy a part of the data on screen and paste it directly into a spreadsheet. The text data on various government agencies from the U.S. Census Bureau is shown in **Figure 2.12**. Notice that some of the data packed together at the beginning needs to be separated into columns.

Figure 2.12

2007 Governments Integrated Directory

```
2007gid_counties - Notepad
File  Edit  Format  View  Help
01100100100000AUTAUGA              COUNTY
01100700700000BUTLER               COUNTY
01101101100000CHILTON              COUNTY
01101801800000CONECUH              COUNTY
01102302300000DALE                 COUNTY
01103603600000JACKSON              COUNTY
01104004000000LAWRENCE             COUNTY
01104704700000MARION               COUNTY
01105405400000PICKENS              COUNTY
01106506500000WASHINGTON           COUNTY
01103103100000GENEVA               COUNTY
03100800800000MOHAVE               COUNTY
```

- *Delimited files.* These have punctuation marks—commas, semi-colons, tabs—between each column of information and often have file extensions of .csv; spreadsheets and database managers can usually open them easily. For example, see the information shown in **Figure 2.13**, which, in this case, is tuberculosis data for the world.

Figure 2.13

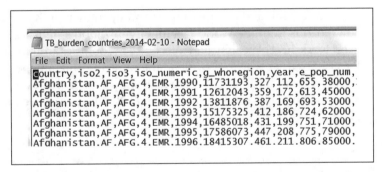

```
TB_burden_countries_2014-02-10 - Notepad
File  Edit  Format  View  Help
country,iso2,iso3,iso_numeric,g_whoregion,year,e_pop_num,
Afghanistan,AF,AFG,4,EMR,1990,11731193,327,112,655,38000,
Afghanistan,AF,AFG,4,EMR,1991,12612043,359,172,613,45000,
Afghanistan,AF,AFG,4,EMR,1992,13811876,387,169,693,53000,
Afghanistan,AF,AFG,4,EMR,1993,15175325,412,186,724,62000,
Afghanistan,AF,AFG,4,EMR,1994,16485018,431,199,751,71000,
Afghanistan,AF,AFG,4,EMR,1995,17586073,447,208,775,79000,
Afghanistan,AF,AFG,4,EMR,1996,18415307,461,211,806,85000.
```

- *Portable document format or PDF files.* These are files made for printouts, or otherwise reviewing a static presentation of data, and not for data analysis. They used to be the bane of CAR, but there is now software to convert many of them into spreadsheet format. While they look like other data, as shown in **Figure 2.12** above, they require work to import into spreadsheets or database managers. Fortunately, there are lots of tools to convert PDF files into usable Excel files. (See **Figure 2.14**.)

Figure 2.14

Subject	United States			
	Estimate	Margin of Error	Percent	Percent Margin of Error
HOUSING OCCUPANCY				
Total housing units	132,452,249	+/-3,899	132,452,249	(X)
Occupied housing units	115,969,540	+/-150,555	87.6%	+/-0.1
Vacant housing units	16,482,709	+/-151,760	12.4%	+/-0.1
Homeowner vacancy rate	2.0	+/-0.1	(X)	(X)
Rental vacancy rate	6.8	+/-0.1	(X)	(X)
UNITS IN STRUCTURE				
Total housing units	132,452,249	+/-3,899	132,452,249	(X)
1-unit, detached	81,554,643	+/-96,447	61.6%	+/-0.1
1-unit, attached	7,695,788	+/-39,654	5.8%	+/-0.1
2 units	5,006,114	+/-32,000	3.8%	+/-0.1
3 or 4 units	5,880,296	+/-36,686	4.4%	+/-0.1
5 to 9 units	6,311,130	+/-48,988	4.8%	+/-0.1
10 to 19 units	5,927,271	+/-42,333	4.5%	+/-0.1
20 or more units	11,465,984	+/-45,014	8.7%	+/-0.1
Mobile home	8,510,590	+/-47,407	6.4%	+/-0.1
Boat, RV, van, etc.	100,433	+/-5,010	0.1%	+/-0.1

Downloading Different Files

Let's do several kinds of downloads and open them in Excel. The first download is from the World Health Organization's statistics site of an Excel worksheet of healthy life expectancy in countries around the world. This is the easier way to download the same information we saw in an HTML file in **Figure 2.11**. **Figure 2.15** shows a site that allows you to download the data by clicking on "Excel" on the line above the data.

Figure 2.15

Download this data as										
CSV (codes only) | CSV (text only) | CSV (text and codes) | CSV (XMart) | Excel (SpreadsheetML) | HTML (flat table) | GHO X										
Details: off			Life expectancy at birth (years)			Life expectancy at age 60 (years)			Healthy life expectancy (HALE) at birth (years)	
Country	Year	Male	Female	Both sexes	Male	Female	Both sexes	Male	Female	Both sexes
Afghanistan	2012	58	61	60	15	17	16	49	49	49
	2000	54	56	55	14	16	15	45	45	45
	1990	49	50	49	13	15	14			
Albania	2012	73	75	74	18	20	19	64	66	65
	2000	68	73	70	15	18	17	60	64	62

Clicking on the file causes it to automatically download into Excel, as shown in **Figure 2.16**. You need only save it to the folder where you wish to keep it on your computer; then you can begin your analysis. (You may get a few more columns than show on the Website, but it's the same data.)

Figure 2.16

		Females			Males		
1	Chart CO1.2.C: Life expectancy at birth and Healthy Adjusted Life Expectancy at birth (HALE), in y						
2							
3			sorted					
4		Females			Males		
		Life expectancy	Healthy life expectancy	Diff LE - HALE (in years)	Life expectancy	Healthy life expectancy	Diff LE - HALE (in years)
5	Countries						
6	Japan	86.0	78.0	8.0	79.0	73.0	6.0
7	France	84.0	76.0	8.0	77.0	71.0	6.0
8	Italy 1	84.0	76.0	8.0	79.0	73.0	6.0
9	Spain	84.0	76.0	8.0	78.0	71.0	7.0
10	Switzerland	84.0	76.0	8.0	79.0	73.0	6.0
11	Australia	84.0	75.0	9.0	79.0	72.0	7.0
12	Canada 1	83.0	75.0	8.0	78.0	71.0	7.0
13	Finland	83.0	75.0	8.0	76.0	70.0	6.0
14	Germany	82.0	75.0	7.0	77.0	71.0	6.0

Let's try importing data from an HTML file. In this example, we will copy and paste the database we want from a Website that keeps track of organ transplants. By going to the United Network for Organ Sharing Website (www.unos.org), we find tables with data about the number of persons waiting for transplants by state. (See **Figure 2.17**.)

Figure 2.17

	All Organs	Kidney	Liver	Pancreas	Kidney / Pancreas	Heart	Lung
All States	134,131	108,371	16,401	1,202	2,107	4,029	1,703
Alabama	3,934	3,690	130	14	28	41	28
Arizona	2,526	2,018	373	18	47	56	14
Arkansas	310	259	20	0	0	31	0
California	23,106	19,043	3,095	79	277	357	210
Colorado	2,596	1,788	659	21	35	56	37

As shown in **Figure 2.18**, we highlight the data. Then, right-click and choose "Copy" in the menu bar.

Figure 2.18

		All Organs	Kidney	Liver	Pancreas	Kidney / Pancreas	Heart	Lung	Heart / Lung
All States	I	134,131	108,371	16,401	1,202	2,107	4,029	1,703	56
Alabama	I	3,934	3,690	130	14	28	41	28	3
Arizona	I	2,526	2,018	373	18	47	56	14	0
Arkansas	I	310	259	20	0	0	31	0	0

We open Excel and click on the top box (A1) of the grid. We then right-click and choose "Paste." The data on the waiting list is pasted into the spreadsheet, as in **Figure 2.19**.

Figure 2.19

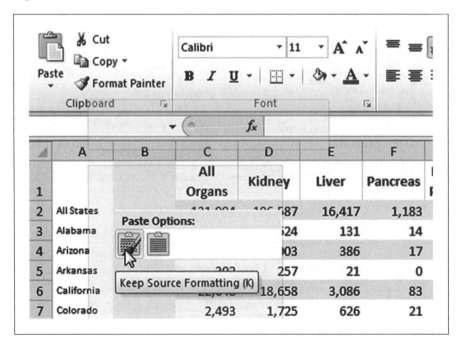

Now, we will get a fixed format file from the Web. We go to the U.S. Census Bureau's Website and choose the data we have seen before—the list of government entities by county. (See **Figure 2.20**.)

Figure 2.20

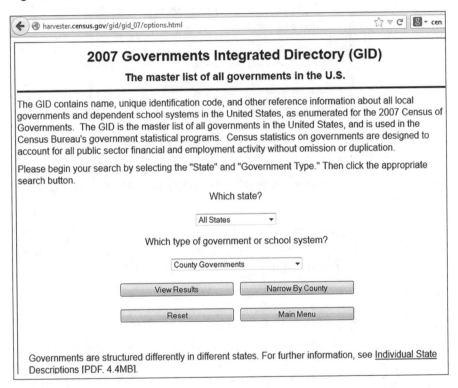

When we click on "View Results," we get a compressed zipped file that generally will open automatically when downloaded, as in **Figure 2.21**.

Figure 2.21

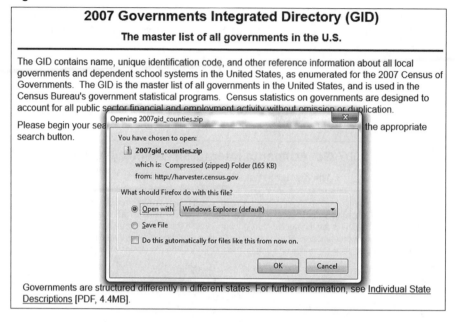

2007 Governments Integrated Directory (GID)

The master list of all governments in the U.S.

The GID contains name, unique identification code, and other reference information about all local governments and dependent school systems in the United States, as enumerated for the 2007 Census of Governments. The GID is the master list of all governments in the United States, and is used in the Census Bureau's government statistical programs. Census statistics on governments are designed to account for all public sector financial and employment activity without omission or duplication.

Please begin your sea... the appropriate search button.

Opening 2007gid_counties.zip

You have chosen to open:

🗎 2007gid_counties.zip

which is: Compressed (zipped) Folder (165 KB)
from: http://harvester.census.gov

What should Firefox do with this file?

◉ Open with   Windows Explorer (default)

○ Save File

☐ Do this automatically for files like this from now on.

OK   Cancel

Governments are structured differently in different states. For further information, see Individual State Descriptions [PDF, 4.4MB].

We click on "OK" and we get two files, as shown in **Figure 2.22**. One file is the data, and one is the layout file, which tells you what columns the information goes in and how wide the columns are.

Figure 2.22

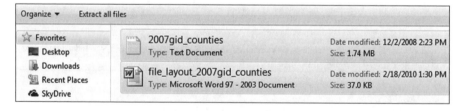

Organize ▼   Extract all files

☆ Favorites
  ▤ Desktop
  🗊 Downloads
  🗎 Recent Places
  ☁ SkyDrive

📄 2007gid_counties
   Type: Text Document
   Date modified: 12/2/2008 2:23 PM
   Size: 1.74 MB

📄 file_layout_2007gid_counties
   Type: Microsoft Word 97 - 2003 Document
   Date modified: 2/18/2010 1:30 PM
   Size: 37.0 KB

When we click on the data file (2007gid_counties.zip), we see it is in fixed format—all of the data is left justified, as in **Figure 2.23**.

Figure 2.23

2007gid_counties - Notepad

File   Edit   Format   View   Help

```
01100100100000AUTAUGA          COUNTY          CHAIRMAN
01100700700000BUTLER           COUNTY          CHAIRMAN
01101101100000CHILTON          COUNTY          CHAIRMAN
01101801800000CONECUH          COUNTY          CHAIRMAN
01102302300000DALE             COUNTY          PROBATE JUDGE
```

In looking at that data we know we are going to need guidelines on how to slice it into columns, and that is what a record layout will do. We will talk about record layouts in later chapters, but this is a good time to see why it is so important to get a layout, as in **Figure 2.24**.

Figure 2.24

FILE LAYOUT FOR 2007gid_counties.txt				
2007 Governments Integrated Directory - Counties				
Field Name	**Positions**	**Start Position**	**Length**	**Characteristic**
State	01-02	01	2	Governments ID - State code 01 - Alabama thru 51 - Wyoming
Type	03-03	03	1	Governments ID - Type of Government code Always '1' (indicates "county government")
County	04-06	04	3	Governments ID - County code Numeric
Unit	07-09	07	3	Governments ID - Unit code Numeric
Supplement	10-12	10	3	Governments ID - Supplement code Always '000' (records are independent governm
Sub Code	13-14	13	2	Governments ID - Sub code Always '00' (records are independent governme
Government Name	15-78	15	64	Name of governmental unit

The record layout tells you how many spaces the data gets in each column. When you import data into a spreadsheet such as Excel, this information is critical to having an accurate download and importing the data into the spreadsheet format. To begin, we keep the record layout open, and we open the data file out of a folder, as in **Figure 2.25**.

Figure 2.25

Documents library

data

Name	Date modified	Type	Size
0713-ffl-list-missouri	1/31/2014 6:09 PM	Text Document	369 KB
0713-ffl-list-missouri	1/31/2014 6:07 PM	Microsoft Excel 97...	912 KB
990layout	11/28/2013 12:40 ...	Text Document	2 KB
2007gid_counties	12/2/2008 3:23 PM	Text Document	1,784 KB

Now comes the tricky part: opening this file with Excel. When we click on "Open" under "File," a wizard screen appears, as in **Figure 2.26**. The wizard notes whether the text is in fixed format or includes delimiters, such as commas.

Figure 2.26

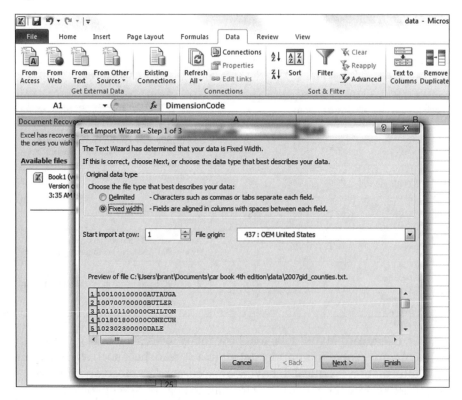

In this case, we choose "Fixed width" because it is a text file in which the columns (also called *fields*) are already left justified and should have spaces in between. When we click "Next," we find that we now can draw the lines in the data to establish columns and can delete or move the lines, as in **Figure 2.27**.

Sometimes Excel guesses the right places to put the lines, but in the beginning part of this data it does not. Therefore, it is up to us to create lines at the correct spaces according to the file record layout, as shown in **Figure 2.28**. That is, "state" is the first two spaces, "type of government" is the third space, "county" is the next three spaces, and so on.

Figure 2.27

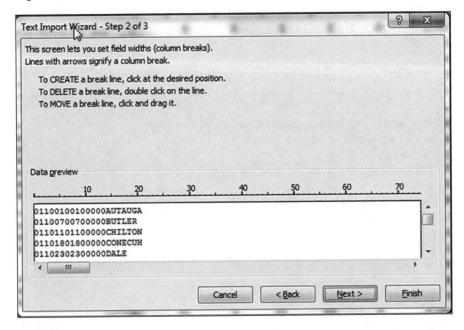

Figure 2.28

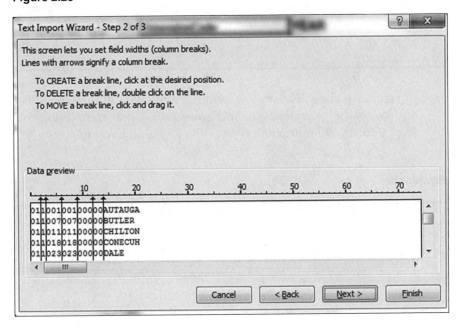

We hit "Next" again, and the wizard now offers us the option to change "Data Format," or data types, as shown in **Figure 2.29**. (We will talk about data types in later chapters.)

Figure 2.29

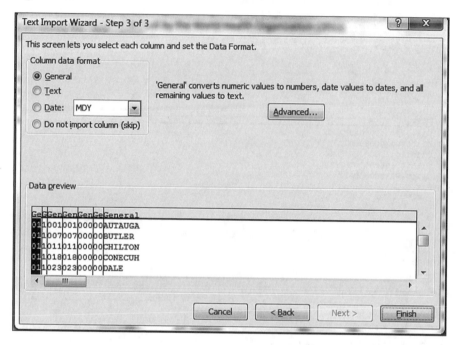

When we click "Finish," we will have the data in the worksheet and be ready for analysis, as in **Figure 2.30**. Upon completing this step, you should immediately save the file as an Excel file.

Figure 2.30

	A	B	C	D	E	F	G	H	I
1	1	1	1	1	0	0	AUTAUGA	COUNTY	CHAIRMAN
2	1	1	7	7	0	0	BUTLER	COUNTY	CHAIRMAN
3	1	1	11	11	0	0	CHILTON	COUNTY	CHAIRMAN
4	1	1	18	18	0	0	CONECUH	COUNTY	CHAIRMAN
5	1	1	23	23	0	0	DALE	COUNTY	PROBATE JUDGE

Next, we will try downloading delimited files of the same information. The standard delimited file is the comma-separated values (CSV) file, and most CSV files are as easy to download into Excel as Excel files. For example, the CSV file on cases of tuberculosis around the world opens automatically in Excel when you download it—that is, as long as you have Excel on your computer. We click on the file on the Web, as in **Figure 2.31.**

Figure 2.31

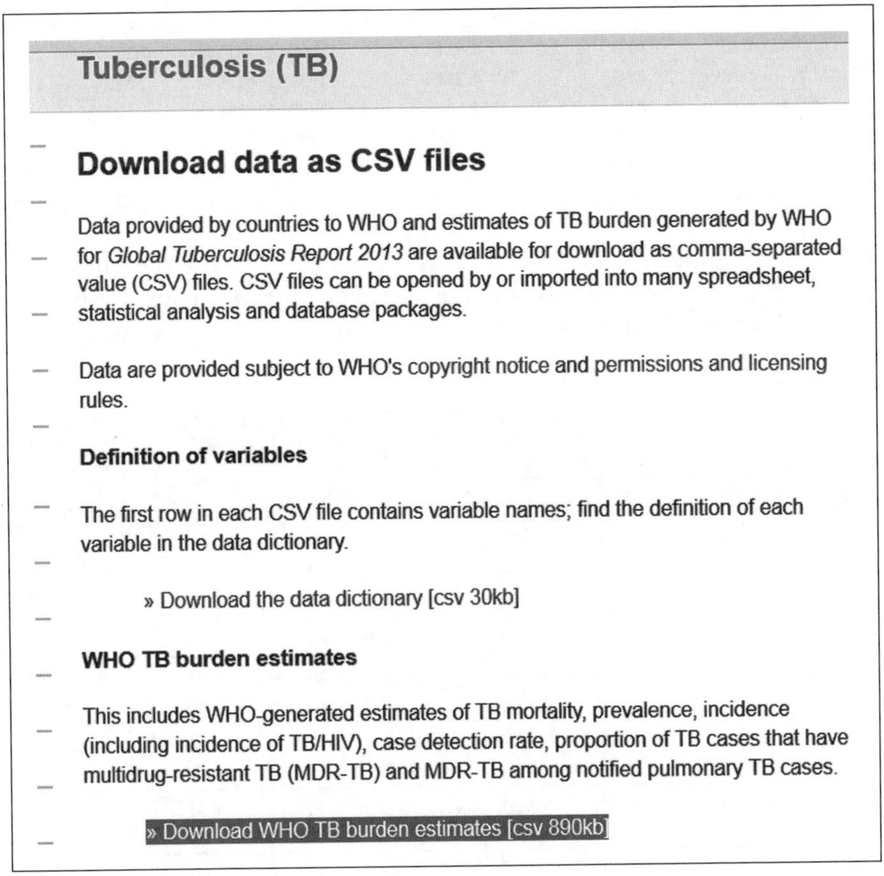

Tuberculosis (TB)

Download data as CSV files

Data provided by countries to WHO and estimates of TB burden generated by WHO for *Global Tuberculosis Report 2013* are available for download as comma-separated value (CSV) files. CSV files can be opened by or imported into many spreadsheet, statistical analysis and database packages.

Data are provided subject to WHO's copyright notice and permissions and licensing rules.

Definition of variables

The first row in each CSV file contains variable names; find the definition of each variable in the data dictionary.

» Download the data dictionary [csv 30kb]

WHO TB burden estimates

This includes WHO-generated estimates of TB mortality, prevalence, incidence (including incidence of TB/HIV), case detection rate, proportion of TB cases that have multidrug-resistant TB (MDR-TB) and MDR-TB among notified pulmonary TB cases.

» Download WHO TB burden estimates [csv 890kb]

When downloaded, the data goes directly into Excel. All you have to do is save it as an Excel file and do your analysis. (See **Figure 2.32.**)

Figure 2.32

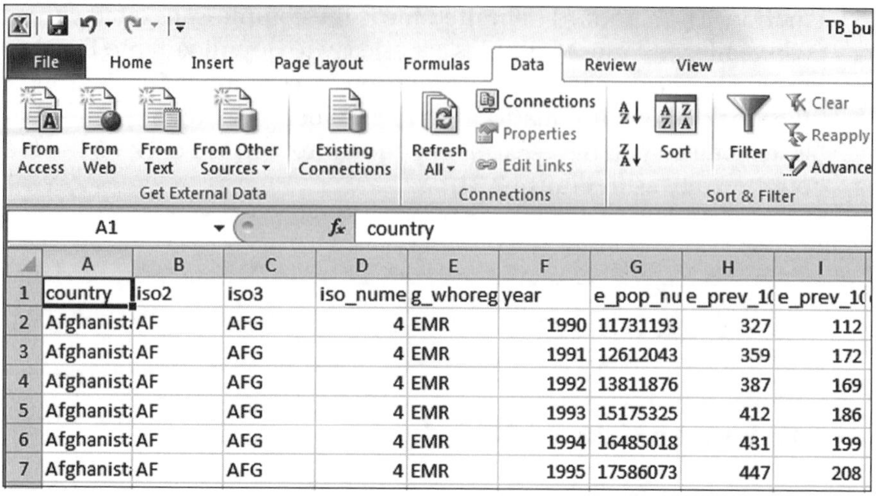

Sometimes, a file will say it is a CSV file, but the delimiters are semicolons, tabs, or other characters. For example, consider the database on gun dealers in the United States shown in **Figure 2.33**.

Figure 2.33

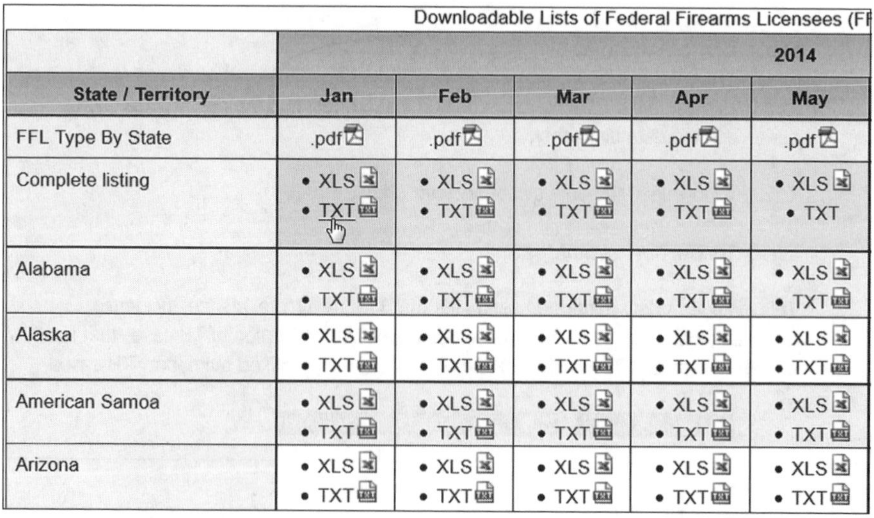

Downloadable Lists of Federal Firearms Licensees (FF					
			2014		
State / Territory	**Jan**	**Feb**	**Mar**	**Apr**	**May**
FFL Type By State	.pdf	.pdf	.pdf	.pdf	.pdf
Complete listing	• XLS • TXT	• XLS • TXT	• XLS • TXT	• XLS • TXT	• XLS • TXT
Alabama	• XLS • TXT	• XLS • TXT	• XLS • TXT	• XLS • TXT	• XLS • TXT
Alaska	• XLS • TXT	• XLS • TXT	• XLS • TXT	• XLS • TXT	• XLS • TXT
American Samoa	• XLS • TXT	• XLS • TXT	• XLS • TXT	• XLS • TXT	• XLS • TXT
Arizona	• XLS • TXT	• XLS • TXT	• XLS • TXT	• XLS • TXT	• XLS • TXT

As you can see, you can download data in several formats. You might download the text file because you want to filter out some kinds of records before downloading the data into Excel or eventually importing it into some other kind of analytical software.

If you did download the data as a .txt file and open it in Excel, you would get the import wizard again; you would want to say the file was delimited. (See **Figure 2.34**.)

Figure 2.34

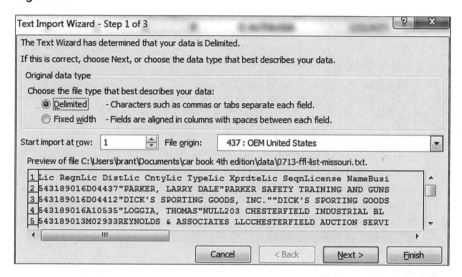

We click "Next" and check what the wizard identifies as the delimiter—in this case, a tab. (See **Figure 2.35**.)

Figure 2.35

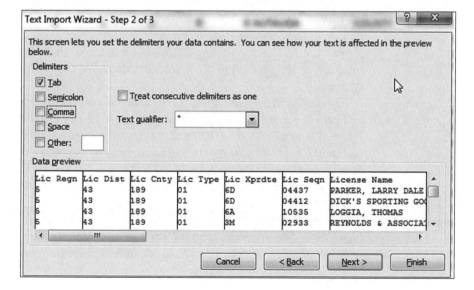

From here, the steps are the same as with the fixed format. We click "Next," and the wizard offers "Data Types" again. We click "Finish," and we have our data in Excel again and are ready to work with the data, as in **Figure 2.36**.

Figure 2.36

	A	B	C	D	E	F	G	
1	Lic Reg	Lic Di	Lic Cnt	Lic Typ	Lic Xprc	Lic Seqn	License Name	Business Name
2	5	43	189	1	6D	4437	PARKER, LARRY DALE	PARKER SAFETY TRA
3	5	43	189	1	6D	4412	DICK'S SPORTING GOODS, INC.	DICK'S SPORTING G(
4	5	43	189	1	6A	10535	LOGGIA, THOMAS	NULL
5	5	43	189	1	3M	2933	REYNOLDS & ASSOCIATES LLC	CHESTERFIELD AUCT
6	5	43	189	10	5B	3769	SENTRUS GOVERNMENT SYSTEMS DIVISION	NULL
7	5	43	189	1	5H	6485	MARCO POLO OUTFITTERS LC	MARCO POLO OUTF

There always is the potential of problems in downloading databases: sometimes the delimiter is misidentified; sometimes there are hidden marks or characters in the data. But if you go slowly and make sure to closely examine the data, you can usually figure out the problem yourself. Once you do that, you are ready do data analysis in pursuit of the good story.

CAR Wars

The Arkansas Democrat-Gazette *embarked on a detailed look at nonprofit, private foundations in Arkansas and found an astounding number. Arkansas's 273 private foundations controlled about $1.5 billion in assets and handed out $116 million in one year. And that's for a state that lags economically behind the rest of the nation. Without the foundations, the impoverished Mississippi River Delta would be even more desperate.*

To understand the foundations' impact, we followed the money and got the 990-PF forms that foundations have to file with the Internal Revenue Service [IRS] and got electronic data from the National Center for Charitable Statistics. But the information goes further. Going online from a desktop computer, we found a large collection of Websites devoted to the nonprofit world in general and foundations in particular.

One information gold mine was the Foundation Center in New York. The organization's Website and its publications were invaluable. At the Foundation Center's Website, you find a foundation's records on gift recipients, foundation officers, and more.

The IRS itself has a plethora of nonprofit related information online, including data files listing all nonprofits. The nonprofit organization Guidestar (www.guidestar.org) collects and posts the information submitted by most nonprofits to the IRS.

Our first story included key statistics on the overall picture of foundations. Our second story focused on the details of the foundation money flowing into the Delta. Our third story looked at the impact of the Walton Family Foundation.

—Jeff Porter, *The Arkansas Democrat-Gazette*

Chapter Checklist

- The Internet can be used for several purposes, including obtaining contacts, doing research, and finding and using databases.
- Listservs, forums, and newsgroups are discussion groups on specific topics.
- Begin every story by checking electronic news archives and using search engines such as Google and Bing.
- Many government Websites have data that can be downloaded for analysis, and many governments have databases on other countries.
- There are several kinds of database formats, all of which can be imported into spreadsheets and database managers with varying levels of difficulty.

Your Turn to Practice

1. Find three international Websites, three federal government Websites, and three state Websites that have data.
2. Download data from one of these sites.
3. Import the data into a spreadsheet.
4. Find a listserv or a news group having to do with CAR, and join it.

3

Spreadsheets, Part 1

Basic Math for Journalists

> *Members of the Virginia General Assembly received more than $117,700 in gifts from businesses, special interest groups, and lobbyists, according to computer-assisted research by Virginia Commonwealth University's [VCU's] Legislative Reporting class. The gifts included hunting trips to Georgia, Texas and even Canada: Two senators hunted caribou in the Arctic Circle, courtesy of the Virginia Sheriffs' Association. The most generous benefactor was Philip Morris, which treated lawmakers to almost $26,000 in meals, entertainment, golf equipment and other freebies. In January, legislators filed reports listing the gifts they received. After creating a database from the reports, VCU students identified the biggest givers and recipients of gifts—and for the first time put the database online so the public can search it.*
>
> —Jeff South, Virginia Commonwealth University

This story, the result of work by a college reporting class of Jeff South, a former reporter and current professor, outdistanced the work by professional journalists and received wide attention in the state of Virginia. It also showed how putting information into a spreadsheet for analysis can lead to powerful stories. South's class collected information on the gifts, entered the 1,000 or so records in a spreadsheet, and did simple calculations to find who was giving gifts to legislators. The resulting stories shed new light on the legislators and those who court them.

Journalists now use spreadsheets daily, whether it is to pick out patterns of waste and abuse in government or to provide context with figures of information that show the years of data and trends. Using spreadsheets is a particularly attractive approach for journalists beginning to do computer-assisted reporting (CAR) because it's easy to get data in a spreadsheet format. As noted in the previous chapter, many government agencies around the world—especially census offices—routinely place data files in spreadsheet format so they can be smoothly downloaded and analyzed.

It is equally easy to enter data in a spreadsheet from documents when no electronic data exists as the VCU students showed. *The Times-Picayune* in New Orleans, for example, entered information on riverboat pilots, taken from their job applications and résumés, to reveal the nepotism, lack of education, and criminal backgrounds among the pilots. In another instance, *USA Today* built a spreadsheet from information revealed in lawsuits to show the abuse and near-enslavement of immigrants.

Becoming Friendly with Numbers

Journalists constantly report on numbers, although you'll often hear them say they hated math in school—and that they still hate it. Well, many people hate flying on airplanes, but they do it because their jobs require them to do so. Not many of these people become pilots, but they know the plane will take them where they need to go.

The same idea applies to modern journalists and spreadsheets. A modern journalist doesn't have to be a mathematician to deal with numbers, but he or she should be willing to use a spreadsheet when needed to get the job done. If not using a spreadsheet, reporters can end up straining for hours with a calculator, trying to figure out whether the mayor has given his cronies the largest raises.

Eric Lipton, a Pulitzer Prize–winning reporter who now works for *The New York Times*, discovered the efficiency of spreadsheets while working at *The Hartford Courant* in Connecticut. Lipton was examining a generous early retirement plan for city employees. He was trying to calculate the percentage of each person's pension as compared to his or her salary at the time of retirement. Experts told him the figure should be approximately 67 percent, but in the city's early retirement plan some retirees' pensions came close to the full amount of their former salary.

Lipton was tediously tapping a calculator for each comparison when he remembered that he had seen a spreadsheet demonstration in which repetitive calculations were done much more rapidly. With a little help, he imported the information into a spreadsheet and learned how to do one calculation. Then he copied that calculation for more than 100 other entries. Those calculations served as the starting point for a front-page story.

What Lipton discovered is that a spreadsheet prevents unnecessary repetition and otherwise saves an enormous amount of time and improves accuracy in calculations. A spreadsheet allows you to quickly figure out such things as who received the most money, who acquired the highest percentage raise, who made the most drug arrests, or which city's housing prices increased the most. Let's take a look at how a spreadsheet can be used for examining pay raises.

You know this year's average raise for city employees is 5 percent. At the same time, you have a list of the mayor's political appointments and their wages last year and this year. (All names in this example are fictional.) Journalists often line up information like this on paper. **Figure 3.1** shows a partial list of the mayor's cronies on the city payroll.

Figure 3.1

Name	Last year	This year
Dee Dale	$45,000	$52,000
Ed Powell	$25,000	$30,000
Jane Deed	$14,000	$19,000
Joe Smith	$30,000	$39,000
Julia Jones	$50,000	$58,000
Mark Forest	$15,000	$21,000
Mary Hill	$22,000	$29,000
Tom Brown	$40,000	$47,000

A spreadsheet takes this idea a step farther. (By the way, the individual boxes in a spreadsheet are called cells.) When a spreadsheet takes in information, it puts it in the kind of grid that **Figure 3.2** shows.

Figure 3.2

	A	B	C
1	Name	Last year	This year
2	Dee Dale	$ 45,000	$ 52,000
3	Ed Powell	$ 25,000	$ 30,000
4	Jane Deed	$ 14,000	$ 19,000
5	Joe Smith	$ 30,000	$ 39,000
6	Julia Jones	$ 50,000	$ 58,000
7	Mark Forest	$ 15,000	$ 21,000
8	Mary Hill	$ 22,000	$ 29,000
9	Tom Brown	$ 40,000	$ 47,000

As you can see in **Figure 3.2**, we now have columns labeled with letters and rows labeled with numbers. This is the key concept of a spreadsheet, and it's one that you have used in other parts of life.

Learning Addresses

If you have ever looked for a town on a hard-copy road atlas, you probably have turned to the index. Let's say that the index refers you to page 7 and identifies the town's location as "D4." You go to page 7. The map is laid out on a grid with letters across the top and numbers down the sides. You look down column D and then look across on row 4 to find the town.

Or perhaps you have played chess and want to replay the game. The instructions for the location of the pieces are also given with letters and numbers defining the squares. A knight, for example, will move from B1 to C4.

Spreadsheets treat your information as though it's part of a map or grid. So in **Figure 3.2** above, the spreadsheet sees Ed Powell's salary not only as $25,000, but also as "B3." So, back to the raises.

Look at the first row of Dee Dale. Dale's salary increased from $45,000 to $52,000. The difference isn't too hard to see. It's $7,000. The changes in others' salaries wouldn't be hard to calculate, although if the mayor had 100 cronies it would start to get taxing (so to speak).

An old-fashioned journalist would analyze raises by taking a calculator and subtracting the information in column B from that in column C. It doesn't take too long to do the calculations for a list of ten or twenty names, but frequently a journalist is handed a list of hundreds or thousands of names. In Lipton's study of pensions and salaries, he had more than 100 names and was not looking happily ahead to hours of work.

This is where a spreadsheet comes in handy. In a spreadsheet, you would not subtract $45,000 from $52,000. You would subtract B2 from C2. But where would you put it? Well, there's a blank space next to C2, called D2. So, here's the way to do it in a spreadsheet:

As **Figure 3.3** shows, move the cursor to box D2 and click on your mouse. Then type "=C2-B2." Always type the equal sign first so that the spreadsheet knows a formula is coming. (Uppercase or lowercase does not matter.)

Figure 3.3

	A	B	C	D
1	Name	Last year	This year	Raise
2	Dee Dale	$ 45,000	$ 52,000	=C2-B2
3	Ed Powell	$ 25,000	$ 30,000	
4	Jane Deed	$ 14,000	$ 19,000	
5	Joe Smith	$ 30,000	$ 39,000	
6	Julia Jones	$ 50,000	$ 58,000	
7	Mark Forest	$ 15,000	$ 21,000	
8	Mary Hill	$ 22,000	$ 29,000	
9	Tom Brown	$ 40,000	$ 47,000	

Hit the "Enter" key, and there, in **Figure 3.4**, is the result: $7,000.

Figure 3.4

	A	B	C	D
1	Name	Last year	This year	
2	Dee Dale	$ 45,000	$ 52,000	$ 7,000
3	Ed Powell	$ 25,000	$ 30,000	
4	Jane Deed	$ 14,000	$ 19,000	
5	Joe Smith	$ 30,000	$ 39,000	
6	Julia Jones	$ 50,000	$ 58,000	
7	Mark Forest	$ 15,000	$ 21,000	
8	Mary Hill	$ 22,000	$ 29,000	
9	Tom Brown	$ 40,000	$ 47,000	

What you just did is set up a formula—not a complicated one—but a formula nonetheless that does the simple arithmetic for you.

Now you're ready to use the spreadsheet to save time. You want to repeat the formula for every raise. Repeat the formula by copying not $7,000 but "=C2-B2." In most spreadsheets, one way to do this is move the cursor back to D2 and highlight the formula by placing the cursor there and clicking on the formula. Highlight D2, and then move the cursor to the lower right-hand corner of D2 until you see a narrow cross, as in **Figure 3.5**.

Figure 3.5

	A	B	C	D
1	Name	Last year	This year	
2	Dee Dale	$ 45,000	$ 52,000	$ 7,000
3	Ed Powell	$ 25,000	$ 30,000	
4	Jane Deed	$ 14,000	$ 19,000	
5	Joe Smith	$ 30,000	$ 39,000	
6	Julia Jones	$ 50,000	$ 58,000	
7	Mark Forest	$ 15,000	$ 21,000	
8	Mary Hill	$ 22,000	$ 29,000	
9	Tom Brown	$ 40,000	$ 47,000	

Next, define or shade the area you want to copy by clicking on D2, holding down the button on your mouse, and dragging the shading to the last row, as in **Figure 3.6**.

Figure 3.6

	A	B	C	D
1	Name	Last year	This year	
2	Dee Dale	$ 45,000	$ 52,000	$ 7,000
3	Ed Powell	$ 25,000	$ 30,000	
4	Jane Deed	$ 14,000	$ 19,000	
5	Joe Smith	$ 30,000	$ 39,000	
6	Julia Jones	$ 50,000	$ 58,000	
7	Mark Forest	$ 15,000	$ 21,000	
8	Mary Hill	$ 22,000	$ 29,000	
9	Tom Brown	$ 40,000	$ 47,000	
10				

Now let go of the clicker on your mouse, and there are all your numbers. (See **Figure 3.7**.)

Figure 3.7

	A	B	C	D	E
	=C2-B2				
	A	B	C	D	E
1	Name	Last year	This year	Raise	
2	Dee Dale	$ 45,000	$ 52,000	$ 7,000	
3	Ed Powell	$ 25,000	$ 30,000	$ 5,000	
4	Jane Deed	$ 14,000	$ 19,000	$ 5,000	
5	Joe Smith	$ 30,000	$ 39,000	$ 9,000	
6	Julia Jones	$ 50,000	$ 58,000	$ 8,000	
7	Mark Forest	$ 15,000	$ 21,000	$ 6,000	
8	Mary Hill	$ 22,000	$ 29,000	$ 7,000	
9	Tom Brown	$ 40,000	$ 47,000	$ 7,000	
10					

What you are doing is telling the spreadsheet to do the same thing it did in D2 for the rest of the rows. Notice that the formula =C2-B2 is shown above the worksheet so that you know what formula was copied.

As we said, the spreadsheet isn't going to copy $7,000 to every box in the D column. It's going to copy the formula of subtracting the B column from the C column in each row. So it will subtract B4 from C4, B5 from C5 and so on.

Always take a close look at the column after you have copied the formula. (We will label new columns later in this chapter.) Some spreadsheets allow you to copy formulas more easily, but sometimes they may "guess" incorrectly at what formula you want to copy. Furthermore, if you did copy your formula incorrectly, you will increase your error by the number of rows you copied it to.

Another way to copy your formula—if there are no blank rows—is to double-click once you see the narrow cross. When you double-click the narrow cross, the formula will be copied and the numbers will be copied and appear until there is a blank row.

Calculating Percentages

Let's continue our analysis of the increases. When you look at the salary increases, the largest increase is not necessarily the most important. After all, $5,000 added to $60,000 doesn't have the same impact as $5,000 added to $30,000. Often, you want to know who received the highest percentage increase. This brings you to a bugaboo of many journalists: the percentage difference.

Calculating a percentage difference is straightforward if you break it down into its components. If one of the mayor's cronies is making $45,000 and gets a raise to $52,000, the difference is $7,000. That means you divide 7,000 (the increase) by 45,000 (the original salary): 7,000/$45,000. That gives you .155, which is the same as 15.5 percent.

If you were saying it instead of calculating it: "Subtract the first column from the second column and divide the result by the first." In this case, it's $52,000 minus $45,000; then $7,000 divided by $45,000. Another way to remember it is what journalists call NOO (new–old/old, or new minus old divided by old). How would this look in a spreadsheet? Go to your spreadsheet and find the difference: $7,000. That's in cell D2. Where's the old salary? In cell B2. So your formula is D2/B2, as **Figure 3.8** shows.

Figure 3.8

	A	B	C	D	E
1	Name	Last year	This year	Raise	
2	Dee Dale	$ 45,000	$ 52,000	$ 7,000	=D2/B2
3	Ed Powell	$ 25,000	$ 30,000	$ 5,000	
4	Jane Deed	$ 14,000	$ 19,000	$ 5,000	
5	Joe Smith	$ 30,000	$ 39,000	$ 9,000	
6	Julia Jones	$ 50,000	$ 58,000	$ 8,000	
7	Mark Forest	$ 15,000	$ 21,000	$ 6,000	
8	Mary Hill	$ 22,000	$ 29,000	$ 7,000	
9	Tom Brown	$ 40,000	$ 47,000	$ 7,000	
10					

Once again, tip off the spreadsheet with the equal sign in box E2, type "D2/B2," hit "Enter," and the result appears, as **Figure 3.9** shows.

Figure 3.9

=D2/B2

	A	B	C	D	E
1	Name	Last year	This year	Raise	
2	Dee Dale	$ 45,000	$ 52,000	$ 7,000	0.1555556
3	Ed Powell	$ 25,000	$ 30,000	$ 5,000	
4	Jane Deed	$ 14,000	$ 19,000	$ 5,000	
5	Joe Smith	$ 30,000	$ 39,000	$ 9,000	
6	Julia Jones	$ 50,000	$ 58,000	$ 8,000	
7	Mark Forest	$ 15,000	$ 21,000	$ 6,000	
8	Mary Hill	$ 22,000	$ 29,000	$ 7,000	
9	Tom Brown	$ 40,000	$ 47,000	$ 7,000	

Again, to save time, copy the formula using the narrow cross. Your result will be as shown in **Figure 3.10**.

Figure 3.10

=D9/B9

	A	B	C	D	E
1	Name	Last year	This year	Raise	
2	Dee Dale	$ 45,000	$ 52,000	$ 7,000	0.1555556
3	Ed Powell	$ 25,000	$ 30,000	$ 5,000	0.2000000
4	Jane Deed	$ 14,000	$ 19,000	$ 5,000	0.3571429
5	Joe Smith	$ 30,000	$ 39,000	$ 9,000	0.3000000
6	Julia Jones	$ 50,000	$ 58,000	$ 8,000	0.1600000
7	Mark Forest	$ 15,000	$ 21,000	$ 6,000	0.4000000
8	Mary Hill	$ 22,000	$ 29,000	$ 7,000	0.3181818
9	Tom Brown	$ 40,000	$ 47,000	$ 7,000	0.1750000
10					
11					

But there are too many numbers to the right of the decimal, and it looks confusing. You would never print or broadcast percentages in this form, so you use a handy icon from the spreadsheet. You highlight the column by clicking on the letter E above the top row, moving the cursor onto the percent (%) sign, and clicking on it, as shown in **Figure 3.11**. (At this point, let's put column labels on the change column and percent column.)

Figure 3.11

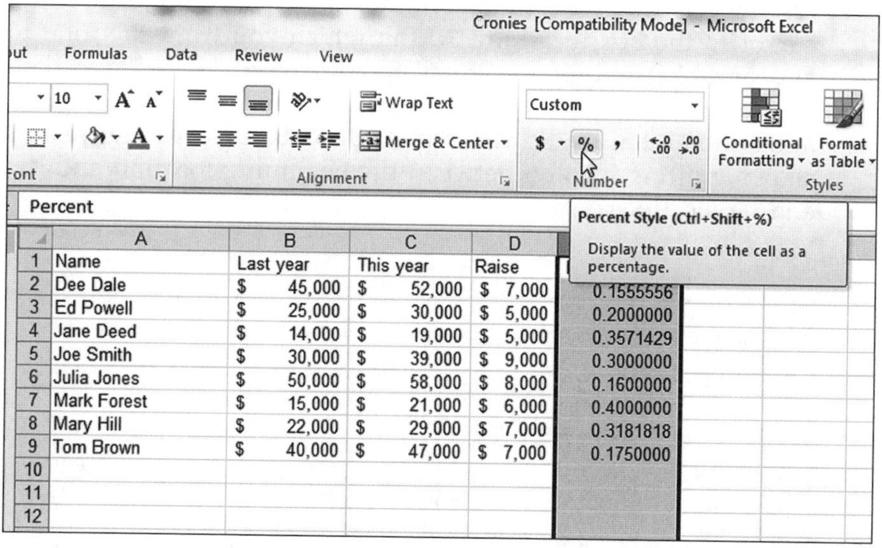

The outcome, as shown in **Figure 3.12**, is much easier to read when you change the numbers into percentages.

Figure 3.12

	A	B	C	D	E
1	Name	Last year	This year	Raise	Percent
2	Dee Dale	$ 45,000	$ 52,000	$ 7,000	16%
3	Ed Powell	$ 25,000	$ 30,000	$ 5,000	20%
4	Jane Deed	$ 14,000	$ 19,000	$ 5,000	36%
5	Joe Smith	$ 30,000	$ 39,000	$ 9,000	30%
6	Julia Jones	$ 50,000	$ 58,000	$ 8,000	16%
7	Mark Forest	$ 15,000	$ 21,000	$ 6,000	40%
8	Mary Hill	$ 22,000	$ 29,000	$ 7,000	32%
9	Tom Brown	$ 40,000	$ 47,000	$ 7,000	18%
10					

Going from Horizontal to Vertical

By comparing rows, you have been doing calculations horizontally in the two-dimensional world of a spreadsheet. But you also can do vertical calculations. For the story on the mayor's cronies, you might want to know how much their salaries are costing taxpayers. For this, you want to total numbers in the columns. Move the cursor to the box in **Figure 3.13** in which you want the total to appear, B11. You type the equal sign, the word "SUM," and then the range of cells you want to total. In this case, the numbers start at B2 and end at B9. So you type "=SUM(B2:B9)," as **Figure 3.13** shows, putting a colon between the beginning location and the ending location.

Figure 3.13

=SUM(B2:B9)

	A	B	C	D	E
1	Name	Last year	This year	Raise	Percent
2	Dee Dale	$ 45,000	$ 52,000	$ 7,000	16%
3	Ed Powell	$ 25,000	$ 30,000	$ 5,000	20%
4	Jane Deed	$ 14,000	$ 19,000	$ 5,000	36%
5	Joe Smith	$ 30,000	$ 39,000	$ 9,000	30%
6	Julia Jones	$ 50,000	$ 58,000	$ 8,000	16%
7	Mark Forest	$ 15,000	$ 21,000	$ 6,000	40%
8	Mary Hill	$ 22,000	$ 29,000	$ 7,000	32%
9	Tom Brown	$ 40,000	$ 47,000	$ 7,000	18%
10					
11	Total	=SUM(B2:B9)			
12					

When you hit "Enter," the total appears, as in **Figure 3.14**.

Figure 3.14

	A	B	C	D	E
1	Name	Last year	This year	Raise	Percent
2	Dee Dale	$ 45,000	$ 52,000	$ 7,000	16%
3	Ed Powell	$ 25,000	$ 30,000	$ 5,000	20%
4	Jane Deed	$ 14,000	$ 19,000	$ 5,000	36%
5	Joe Smith	$ 30,000	$ 39,000	$ 9,000	30%
6	Julia Jones	$ 50,000	$ 58,000	$ 8,000	16%
7	Mark Forest	$ 15,000	$ 21,000	$ 6,000	40%
8	Mary Hill	$ 22,000	$ 29,000	$ 7,000	32%
9	Tom Brown	$ 40,000	$ 47,000	$ 7,000	18%
10					
11	Total	$ 241,000			

Rather than repeating the formula for each column, do what you did when calculating differences in rows: using the narrow cross, copy the formula horizontally, as shown in **Figure 3.15**. Remember not to include the percentage column because you are not adding percentages.

Figure 3.15

=SUM(B2:B9)

◢	A	B	C	D	E
1	Name	Last year	This year	Raise	Percent
2	Dee Dale	$ 45,000	$ 52,000	$ 7,000	16%
3	Ed Powell	$ 25,000	$ 30,000	$ 5,000	20%
4	Jane Deed	$ 14,000	$ 19,000	$ 5,000	36%
5	Joe Smith	$ 30,000	$ 39,000	$ 9,000	30%
6	Julia Jones	$ 50,000	$ 58,000	$ 8,000	16%
7	Mark Forest	$ 15,000	$ 21,000	$ 6,000	40%
8	Mary Hill	$ 22,000	$ 29,000	$ 7,000	32%
9	Tom Brown	$ 40,000	$ 47,000	$ 7,000	18%
10					
11	Total	$ 241,000			
12					

Let go of the mouse button, and the result appears, as **Figure 3.16** shows.

Figure 3.16

=SUM(B2:B9)

◢	A	B	C	D	E
1	Name	Last year	This year	Raise	Percent
2	Dee Dale	$ 45,000	$ 52,000	$ 7,000	16%
3	Ed Powell	$ 25,000	$ 30,000	$ 5,000	20%
4	Jane Deed	$ 14,000	$ 19,000	$ 5,000	36%
5	Joe Smith	$ 30,000	$ 39,000	$ 9,000	30%
6	Julia Jones	$ 50,000	$ 58,000	$ 8,000	16%
7	Mark Forest	$ 15,000	$ 21,000	$ 6,000	40%
8	Mary Hill	$ 22,000	$ 29,000	$ 7,000	32%
9	Tom Brown	$ 40,000	$ 47,000	$ 7,000	18%
10					
11	Total	$ 241,000	$ 295,000	$ 54,000	
12					

You might also want to determine how the average increase for the mayor's cronies compares to the average increase for all employees. There are two ways of looking at this. To compare the average percentage increase for the mayor's cronies, giving equal weight to each employee regardless of salary, you would average the percentages in column E and get 26 percent. (We will do an average later in this chapter.)

But if you wanted to calculate the percentage increase in the total amount of money paid to the cronies, you would calculate the difference in the rows. To do that, you would not average the percentages. You would calculate the percentage difference between the totals (C11 and B11) by subtracting B11 from C11 with the answer appearing in D11. Then, you would divide D11 by B11. The result, as **Figure 3.17** shows, would be approximately 22 percent, or more than four times that of all employees, who received at best a 5 percent increase.

Figure 3.17

=D11/B11

	A	B	C	D	E
1	Name	Last year	This year	Raise	Percent
2	Dee Dale	$ 45,000	$ 52,000	$ 7,000	16%
3	Ed Powell	$ 25,000	$ 30,000	$ 5,000	20%
4	Jane Deed	$ 14,000	$ 19,000	$ 5,000	36%
5	Joe Smith	$ 30,000	$ 39,000	$ 9,000	30%
6	Julia Jones	$ 50,000	$ 58,000	$ 8,000	16%
7	Mark Forest	$ 15,000	$ 21,000	$ 6,000	40%
8	Mary Hill	$ 22,000	$ 29,000	$ 7,000	32%
9	Tom Brown	$ 40,000	$ 47,000	$ 7,000	18%
10					
11	Total	$ 241,000	$ 295,000	$54,000	22%

Comparing Parts to the Sum

You might also want to see who got the biggest chunk of money out of the salary increases. If this were a city budget, you might want to see which department received the largest portion of the city budget. In either case, you want to compare the individual raises with the total amount of raises for each person. Thus, you want to compare D2 with D11, D3 with D11, and so on.

However, a spreadsheet is used to moving down a row at each calculation. Without some hint of what you want to do, the spreadsheet will compare D2 with D11 and then D3 with D12, which would be nonsense. The long and short of it is that we need to "anchor" D11.

Fortunately, spreadsheets give us an easy way to accomplish that. As **Figure 3.18** shows, we anchor D11 by putting a dollar sign before the letter and a dollar sign before the number: "$D$11." The first dollar sign anchors the column, and the second dollar sign anchors the row. Now the spreadsheet knows to compare all the numbers in a column only with D11.

Figure 3.18

=D2/$D$11

	A	B	C	D	E	F
1	Name	Last year	This year	Raise	Percent	Percent of Total
2	Dee Dale	$ 45,000	$ 52,000	$ 7,000	16%	=D2/$D$11
3	Ed Powell	$ 25,000	$ 30,000	$ 5,000	20%	
4	Jane Deed	$ 14,000	$ 19,000	$ 5,000	36%	
5	Joe Smith	$ 30,000	$ 39,000	$ 9,000	30%	
6	Julia Jones	$ 50,000	$ 58,000	$ 8,000	16%	
7	Mark Forest	$ 15,000	$ 21,000	$ 6,000	40%	
8	Mary Hill	$ 22,000	$ 29,000	$ 7,000	32%	
9	Tom Brown	$ 40,000	$ 47,000	$ 7,000	18%	
10						
11	Total	$ 241,000	$ 295,000	$ 54,000	22%	

Tap the "Enter" key, and in **Figure 3.19** you obtain a new percentage of the total. (Make sure to format the column as percentages, as you did before.)

Figure 3.19

=D2/$D$11

	A	B	C	D	E	F
1	Name	Last year	This year	Raise	Percent	Percent of Total
2	Dee Dale	$ 45,000	$ 52,000	$ 7,000	16%	13%
3	Ed Powell	$ 25,000	$ 30,000	$ 5,000	20%	
4	Jane Deed	$ 14,000	$ 19,000	$ 5,000	36%	
5	Joe Smith	$ 30,000	$ 39,000	$ 9,000	30%	
6	Julia Jones	$ 50,000	$ 58,000	$ 8,000	16%	
7	Mark Forest	$ 15,000	$ 21,000	$ 6,000	40%	
8	Mary Hill	$ 22,000	$ 29,000	$ 7,000	32%	
9	Tom Brown	$ 40,000	$ 47,000	$ 7,000	18%	
10						
11	Total	$ 241,000	$ 295,000	$ 54,000	22%	

Again, copy the formula. **Figure 3.20** shows the result.

Figure 3.20

	A	B	C	D	E	F
		Jce Smith				
1	Name	Last year	This year	Raise	Percent	Percent of Total
2	Dee Dale	$ 45,000	$ 52,000	$ 7,000	16%	13%
3	Ed Powell	$ 25,000	$ 30,000	$ 5,000	20%	9%
4	Jane Deed	$ 14,000	$ 19,000	$ 5,000	36%	9%
5	Joe Smith	$ 30,000	$ 39,000	$ 9,000	30%	17%
6	Julia Jones	$ 50,000	$ 58,000	$ 8,000	16%	15%
7	Mark Forest	$ 15,000	$ 21,000	$ 6,000	40%	11%
8	Mary Hill	$ 22,000	$ 29,000	$ 7,000	32%	13%
9	Tom Brown	$ 40,000	$ 47,000	$ 7,000	18%	13%
10						
11	Total	$ 241,000	$ 295,000	$ 54,000	22%	
12						

From this calculation you see that Joe Smith got the biggest chunk—17 percent—of the raises.

Sorting the Results

Journalists generally want to analyze and present information in some specific order. If you were doing this with a large spreadsheet, you would have to go through hundreds of numbers to search for the highest percentage. Instead, a spreadsheet allows you to sort the information rapidly.

This brings us to another bugaboo. When you sort the information in a spreadsheet, you want to keep all of the information in each row together. But a spreadsheet can make sorting so easy that a journalist can rush past this important point. Many older versions of spreadsheets allowed you to sort one column of information without moving the rest of the row. That meant your percentages were suddenly scrambled and matched against the wrong information. In newer versions, you can get into the same kind of trouble by putting blank columns between columns of information and ignoring the warnings that pop up.

Before sorting, you must make sure that you outline the entire area to sort. All applicable rows and columns of numbers are highlighted. Here you outline the entire area, as **Figure 3.21** shows.

Figure 3.21

	A	B	C	D	E	F
1	Name	Last year	This year	Raise	Percent	Percent of Total
2	Dee Dale	$ 45,000	$ 52,000	$ 7,000	16%	13%
3	Ed Powell	$ 25,000	$ 30,000	$ 5,000	20%	9%
4	Jane Deed	$ 14,000	$ 19,000	$ 5,000	36%	9%
5	Joe Smith	$ 30,000	$ 39,000	$ 9,000	30%	17%
6	Julia Jones	$ 50,000	$ 58,000	$ 8,000	16%	15%
7	Mark Forest	$ 15,000	$ 21,000	$ 6,000	40%	11%
8	Mary Hill	$ 22,000	$ 29,000	$ 7,000	32%	13%
9	Tom Brown	$ 40,000	$ 47,000	$ 7,000	18%	13%
10						
11	Total	$ 241,000	$ 295,000	$ 54,000	22%	
12						

You then decide to go to the "Sort" command under "Data" in the menu (see **Figure 3.22**).

Figure 3.22

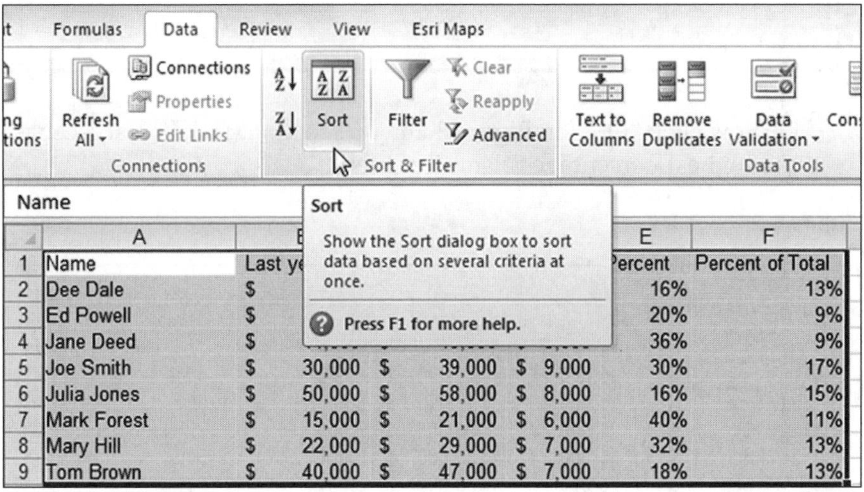

Clicking on "Sort" brings up the next screen, which allows you to choose which column to sort by and in what order. Lowest to highest is called *ascending*, and highest to lowest is called *descending*.

As **Figure 3.23** shows, you choose the "Raise" column and choose "largest to smallest." Note the small box on the top right that says "My data has headers." This means the sort takes into account whether or not you have included the label for each column.

Figure 3.23

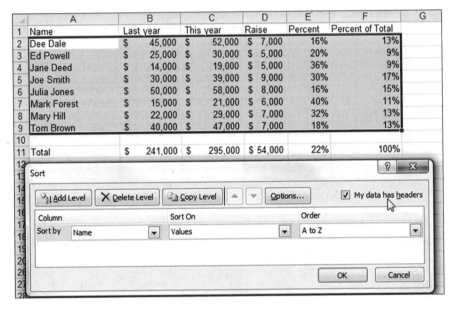

Now click "OK." In **Figure 3.24** you see that Mark Forest received the highest percentage raise, 40 percent.

Figure 3.24

	A	B	C	D	E	F
	Mark Forest					
1	Name	Last year	This year	Raise	Percent	Percent of Total
2	Mark Forest	$ 15,000	$ 21,000	$ 6,000	40%	11%
3	Jane Deed	$ 14,000	$ 19,000	$ 5,000	36%	9%
4	Mary Hill	$ 22,000	$ 29,000	$ 7,000	32%	13%
5	Joe Smith	$ 30,000	$ 39,000	$ 9,000	30%	17%
6	Ed Powell	$ 25,000	$ 30,000	$ 5,000	20%	9%
7	Tom Brown	$ 40,000	$ 47,000	$ 7,000	18%	13%
8	Julia Jones	$ 50,000	$ 58,000	$ 8,000	16%	15%
9	Dee Dale	$ 45,000	$ 52,000	$ 7,000	16%	13%
10						
11	Total	$ 241,000	$ 295,000	$ 54,000	22%	
12						

At this point, your initial work is done, and it's time to start planning your interviews with the mayor, the mayor's cronies, and the regular employees of the city. At the same time, you should start planning your graphics and photos to go with the story.

Using Average and Median for Better Accuracy

To deal with numbers, you should know three of the most common ways of summarizing a collection of numbers: mean, median, and mode. *Mean* is what is commonly called the average. *Median* is defined as the middle value, or the point at which half the numbers fall above and half the numbers fall below. (If there is a tie, it gets a little tricky, but a spreadsheet can work out the calculation for you.) *Mode* is the value that most frequently appears in the database or the value seen the most when you look at data.

Neill Borowski, who practiced and taught CAR at *The Philadelphia Inquirer*, used a good example of this at a national conference. He said baseball players' salaries outraged fans because fans always heard the average salary was $1.2 million. But the median salary was $500,000, and the mode, or the most frequent salary, was $109,000.

Those numbers indicate that there are a few players making really big money. The median, or middle, value, the salary amount that half the salaries exceed and half the salaries fall below, was $500,000. If you asked all baseball players for a count of hands for each salary, the largest number (the mode, not the majority) of hands would go up for $109,000. (Okay, it's still a great deal, but not as much as you thought. And it's being made by people generally making most of their money in ten years or less.)

Journalists want to make sure they represent numbers as fairly and accurately as possible, and these three ways of looking at numbers give them a chance to do so. If a journalist obtains a set of salaries, house prices, or test scores, he or she needs to consider what the fairest representation is. If the numbers are relatively close together, the mean (or average) is a reasonable way to summarize them. But if the numbers are spread out, a journalist doesn't want a few bad apples, or very rich apples, to distort the summary.

Let's stay on the subject of sports and take a look at a National Basketball Association team, the Miami Heat, when superstar LeBron James played for them. (You could select any names for this example.) **Figure 3.25** shows what the players make (a fictional amount).

Figure 3.25

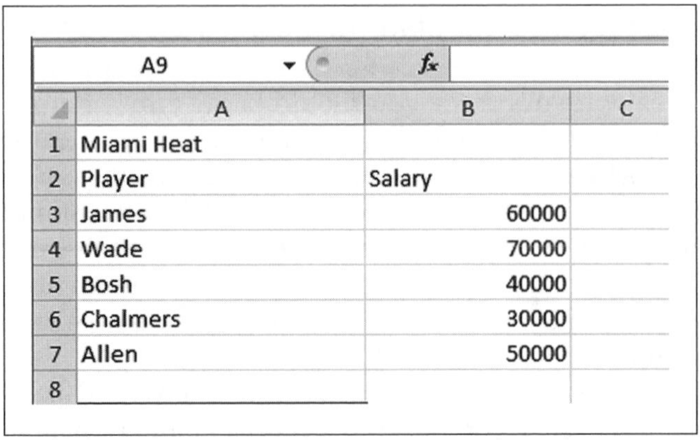

First, we will get the average of what they make. You get an average by going to B8 and typing the formula =AVERAGE(B3:B7), as shown in **Figure 3.26**, and hitting "Enter."

Figure 3.26

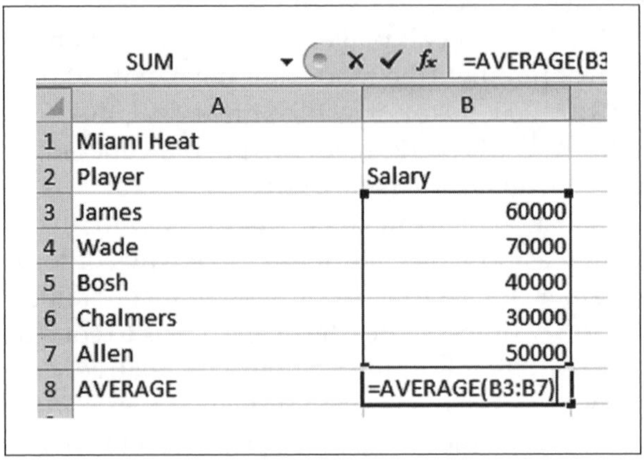

Next, we will get the median of what they make. You obtain a median by going to B9 and typing the formula =MEDIAN(B3:B8), as shown in **Figure 3.27**.

Figure 3.27

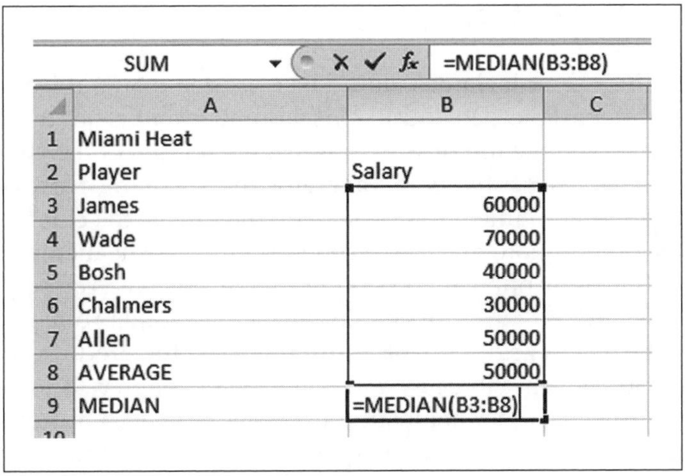

SUM	▾ ⊙ ✕ ✔ *fx*	=MEDIAN(B3:B8)	
◢	A	B	C
1	Miami Heat		
2	Player	Salary	
3	James	60000	
4	Wade	70000	
5	Bosh	40000	
6	Chalmers	30000	
7	Allen	50000	
8	AVERAGE	50000	
9	MEDIAN	=MEDIAN(B3:B8)	
10			

At this point, there is no difference between average and median because there are two salaries higher than $50,000 and two salaries lower than $50,000. Now, let's say we look back at our figures and realize we left a zero off the superstar's salary. We replace James's $60,000 with $600,000, as in **Figure 3.28**.

Figure 3.28

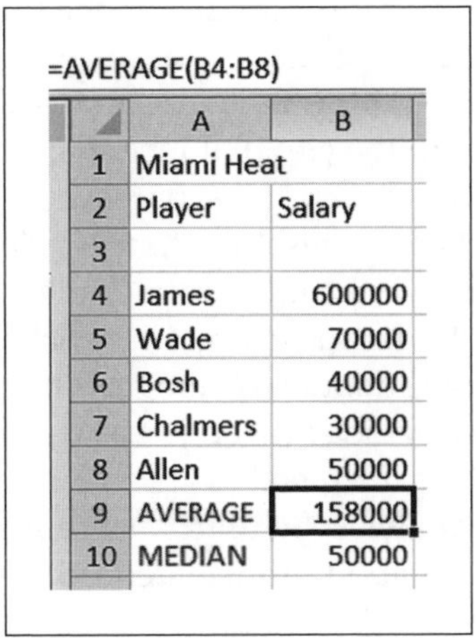

=AVERAGE(B4:B8)		
◢	A	B
1	Miami Heat	
2	Player	Salary
3		
4	James	600000
5	Wade	70000
6	Bosh	40000
7	Chalmers	30000
8	Allen	50000
9	AVERAGE	158000
10	MEDIAN	50000

Notice how the formula immediately changes the resulting average. The median does not change because there are still two salaries higher and two salaries lower than $50,000. This is an extreme example, but you can see that the median more fairly represents what the players make.

Interpreting Outliers

In this example, James would be considered an outlier. In social research parlance, an "outlier" is a number that is out on the edge, or way up on the top or way down at the bottom of the chart.

These measurements—average and median—help you quickly identify an outlier. You could say that James, the chief executive of the corporation, makes ten times as much as the median wage.

But, quite often, if you examine a few databases closely, you begin to regard outliers with healthy suspicion. Outliers often are too good to be true. They frequently turn out to be the product of data-entry errors (which will be examined in a later chapter). The usual disappointment is that someone put in an extra zero, for example, and James's game salary actually is $60,000.

Also, social researchers suggest that you look carefully at the outliers and possibly discard them, especially if you expect to work with averages. That doesn't mean you can't bring the outliers back for a repeat performance later. You might be looking at U.S. Census data and notice that one county has highly unusual numbers. So you first examine the data for all of the counties except for that one in your first analysis. Then, you look at the data for all of the counties together to see how that one county can distort the numbers.

Averages can also hide important information. At the *San Jose Mercury News* in California, in a classic story, reporters obtained an electronic file from the city that included the times of the alarms and the times of fire trucks' arrival at the scene of fires. The fire department claimed that its average response time was four and a half minutes, half a minute under the maximum time it allowed to get to any fire.

Reporters Betty Barnacle and Chris Schmitt found the fire department wasn't wrong about its average. What the fire department didn't say—but the numbers showed—was that on one-fourth of its calls, the fire department exceeded its five-minute maximum response time. With his analysis, Schmitt ensured that the story not only related information about an isolated occurrence, but also showed a pattern of problems.

CAR Wars

When a court reporter at The Hartford Courant, *Jack Ewing, and I looked at racial disparities in bail for criminal defendants in Connecticut, we examined the average bail for blacks and Hispanics versus whites. However, on the advice of some good social science researchers, we limited the bail to amounts above zero and equal to or below $100,000. (We got rid of zero because that meant the person did not have any bail set. We held to $100,000 or below because there were a few amounts above $100,000 that could distort the results.) We found that black and Hispanic males, on average, received much higher bail—nearly double—than whites for the same kind of felony. Then, we went back and looked at the outliers. It turned out that an unusual number of high bail amounts were being given to blacks in one courthouse. In fact, blacks were getting higher bail amounts—as much as $1,000,000—for drug charges than some whites were getting for drug charges or murder.*

Later, a judge in New Haven acknowledged that he was giving out high bail to those accused of drug offenses because he didn't think the accused spent enough time in jail once they were convicted. Thus, his solution was to lock up the presumed innocent. Unfortunately, the judge was contributing to his own frustration because when he kept people in jail awaiting trial, it created prison overcrowding—which led to the early release of those found guilty and serving time. He was unaware, however, that he also was creating racial disparities.

Once again, we learned how numbers and math can not only provide context, but also can tip us to a good stories. Using a spreadsheet to do a few calculations, it's possible to find patterns, make better comparisons, and discover the unusual.

—Brant Houston

Chapter Checklist

- Spreadsheets can help you do calculations faster and more easily.
- Spreadsheets use letters to identify columns and numbers to identify rows.
- When you sort, make sure to highlight the entire range of numbers that you want to sort.

- For calculations, spreadsheets allow you to use column letters and row numbers to create formulas.
- When you are comparing the parts of a calculation with the sum, don't forget to anchor the sum.
- Percentage difference often provides a more fair comparison between the actual change in numbers.
- Take into consideration the best figure to use—mean, median, or mode. And don't forget about the impact of any outliers on your calculation.

Your Turn to Practice

1. Get a list of names and salaries from your city, county, or state in electronic form or in hard copy.
2. Also get a part of a city, county, or state budget in electronic form or in hard copy. Make sure you get two years' worth.
3. Put one or both data sets into a Microsoft Excel worksheet.
4. Sort in descending order using the salary. Sort in descending order using the amount of each budget.
5. Calculate the difference in the budget years. Calculate the percentage difference.
6. Calculate the total, average, and median for the salaries.
7. Find out which department receives the largest percentage of the budget.

Spreadsheets, Part 2

More Math that Matters

We decided to obtain a list of the delinquent taxpayers, analyze it and publish it in a format that people could understand. . . . [T]he top 10 real estate debtors combined owed more than $6.4 million but the city is unlikely to collect any of that soon.

—*The Waterbury Republican American,*
Connecticut

Simply summing the two columns showed what the campaign spent and took in. . . . Overall we found at least $10,000 in unaccounted funds and several violations of state election law.

—*The Courier-Post,* New Jersey

Simply put, a ratio study compares assessed values with actual prices properties sell for. . . . We got a county overseer to admit that his assessors were murmuring privately about "so many mistakes . . . it's unbelievable."

—*The Pittsburgh Tribune-Review,* Pennsylvania

In recent years, journalists have gone beyond the basic math. They calculate a rate and a ratio; filter and reconfigure data to make it more meaningful; and visualize using charts and graphs. Most often, they do this using spreadsheet software, including the more advanced versions of Excel.

Journalists also are using statistical software, such as SPSS, SAS, or R (also called GNU S), and applying the social research methods espoused by Philip Meyer, a pioneer in database analysis and author of *Precision Journalism.*

In the previous chapter, we looked at the basic math a journalist needs to know and how spreadsheets make doing that math faster and easier. This chapter will expand on the basic math and statistics skills for achieving better journalism.

Rates

Sarah Cohen, a Pulitzer Prize–winning reporter and former government statistics expert, says, "Rates are used to level the playing field."

Rates allow you to make comparisons that are more fair and accurate—just as calculations of the median or percentage difference do. Just comparing raw numbers can wrongly and unfairly distort the differences on such topics as illnesses, traffic accidents, and crimes. Ten traffic accidents in an intersection in which only 100 cars pass through a day has a far different impact than ten traffic accidents at an intersection in which 10,000 cars pass a day. Consequently, journalists now calculate rates on many topics such as transportation accidents, taxes, deaths, loans, arrests, and disease. Let's take a look at crime data as an example.

If you were to look at 2012 crime statistics on murder in cities larger than 250,000 in population, it might surprise you to learn that Chicago leads, with 500 murders, and New York is close behind, with 419 (see **Figure 4.1**). After all, Chicago is a city with more than 2.7 million people, and New York has the largest population with more than 8.2 million people.

Figure 4.1

C2		f_x	500	
	A		B	C
1	City		Population	Murders
2	Chicago		2,708,382	500
3	New York		8,289,415	419
4	Detroit		707,096	386
5	Philadelphia		1,538,957	331
6	Los Angeles		3,855,122	299
7	Baltimore		625,474	218
8	Houston		2,177,273	217
9	New Orleans		362,874	193
10	Dallas		1,241,549	154

But would that really tell you how dangerous Chicago is as compared to other cities? Would it give you an idea of the relative chances of being murdered in Chicago as compared to another city? Not really. One way to get a better idea is to use a per capita figure or a rate. Now that you know formulas, you know how easy it is to do a calculation in a spreadsheet.

In **Figure 4.2**, you divide the number of murders in each city (C2 for Chicago) by each city's population (B2). This would give you a per capita (per person) figure; however, all of those decimal places would prevent it from being meaningful to a reader or viewer.

Figure 4.2

D2		f_x =C2/B2		
	A	**B**	**C**	**D**
1	City	Population	Murders	
2	Chicago	2,708,382	500	0.00018
3	New York	8,289,415	419	
4	Detroit	707,096	386	
5	Philadelphia	1,538,957	331	
6	Los Angeles	3,855,122	299	
7	Baltimore	625,474	218	
8	Houston	2,177,273	217	
9	New Orleans	362,874	193	
10	Dallas	1,241,549	154	

To make it more understandable, you need to move the decimal point to the right. You can do this by multiplying the per capita figure by 100,000 to get the rate per 100,000 persons. The multiplier is often a judgment on what makes sense, such as the population size and the number of occurrences in relation to the population (see **Figure 4.3**).

Figure 4.3

SUM		X ✓ f_x =C2/B2*100000			
	A	**B**	**C**	**D**	**E**
1	City	Population	Murders		
2	Chicago	2,708,382	500	=C2/B2*100000	
3	New York	8,289,415	419		
4	Detroit	707,096	386		
5	Philadelphia	1,538,957	331		
6	Los Angeles	3,855,122	299		

Then, by multiplying by 100,000, you get 18.46121, as shown in **Figure 4.4**.

Figure 4.4

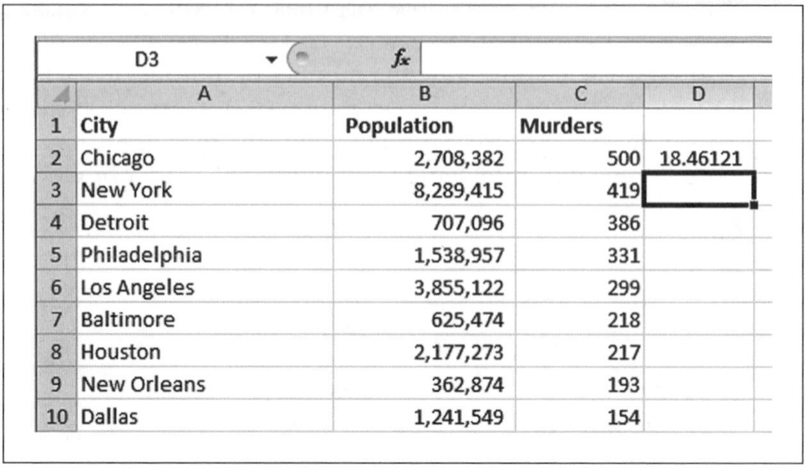
D3
fx

	A	B	C	D
1	City	Population	Murders	
2	Chicago	2,708,382	500	18.46121
3	New York	8,289,415	419	
4	Detroit	707,096	386	
5	Philadelphia	1,538,957	331	
6	Los Angeles	3,855,122	299	
7	Baltimore	625,474	218	
8	Houston	2,177,273	217	
9	New Orleans	362,874	193	
10	Dallas	1,241,549	154	

After you get the formula, copy it down the column with the narrow cross to obtain figures for each city (see **Figure 4.5**). (A helpful hint: Also, click on the comma in the toolbar to reduce the decimals to only two places. This should automatically appear in your toolbar, as shown in **Figure 4.5**.)

Figure 4.5

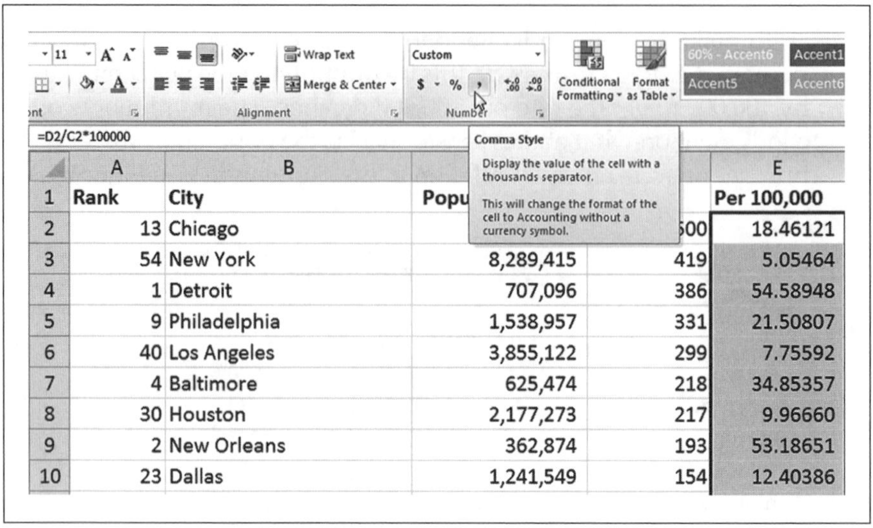
Wrap Text
Merge & Center
Alignment
Custom
Number
Conditional Formatting
Format as Table
60% - Accent6
Accent1
Accent5
Accent6
=D2/C2*100000
Comma Style
Display the value of the cell with a thousands separator.
This will change the format of the cell to Accounting without a currency symbol.

	A	B			E
1	Rank	City	Popu		Per 100,000
2	13	Chicago		500	18.46121
3	54	New York	8,289,415	419	5.05464
4	1	Detroit	707,096	386	54.58948
5	9	Philadelphia	1,538,957	331	21.50807
6	40	Los Angeles	3,855,122	299	7.75592
7	4	Baltimore	625,474	218	34.85357
8	30	Houston	2,177,273	217	9.96660
9	2	New Orleans	362,874	193	53.18651
10	23	Dallas	1,241,549	154	12.40386

Now, sort the information in descending order by the column labeled "Per 100,000," as shown in **Figure 4.6**. (Don't forget to select the entire data range so that columns are not accidentally sorted out of order.)

Figure 4.6

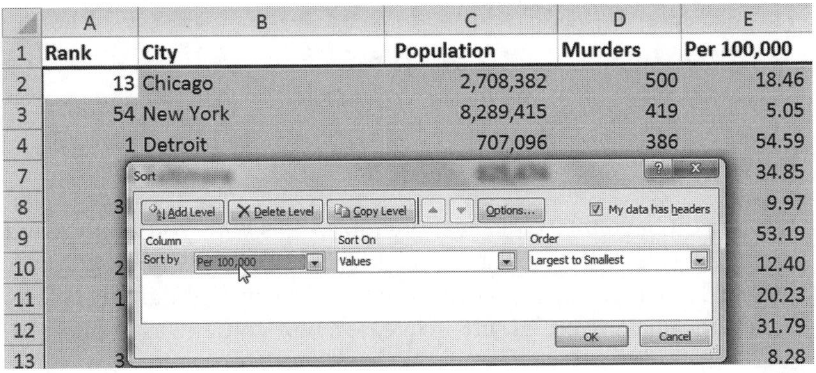

You will find, as shown in **Figures 4.7a** and **4.7b**, that Detroit has the most murders per 100,000 people, at 54.59, Chicago, at 18.46, falls in thirteenth place, and New York's rate is 5.05, which puts it in fifty-fourth place. This gives you some idea of the likelihood of a murder occurring in Detroit as compared to these other cities.

Figure 4.7a

	A	B	C	D
1	City	Population	Murders	Per 100,000
2	Detroit	707,096	386	54.59
3	New Orleans	362,874	193	53.19
4	St. Louis	318,667	113	35.46
5	Baltimore	625,474	218	34.85
6	Newark	278,906	96	34.42
7	Oakland	399,487	127	31.79
8	Stockton	299,105	71	23.74
9	Kansas City	464,073	105	22.63
10	Philadelphia	1,538,957	331	21.51
11	Cleveland	393,781	84	21.33
12	Memphis	657,436	133	20.23
13	Atlanta	437,041	83	18.99
14	Chicago	2,708,382	500	18.46

Figure 4.7b

54	Riverside	313,532	16	5.10
55	New York	8,289,415	419	5.05
56	Anchorage	299,143	15	5.01
57	Virginia Beach	447,588	21	4.69
58	San Jose	976,459	45	4.61
59	Arlington	379,295	17	4.48

Ranking

Once you have the worksheet organized this way, you might want to rank the cities—that is, list the cities from high to low as based on your work. To do this, you first create a new column by highlighting column A and then clicking on "Insert" to create a new column, as in **Figure 4.8**.

Figure 4.8

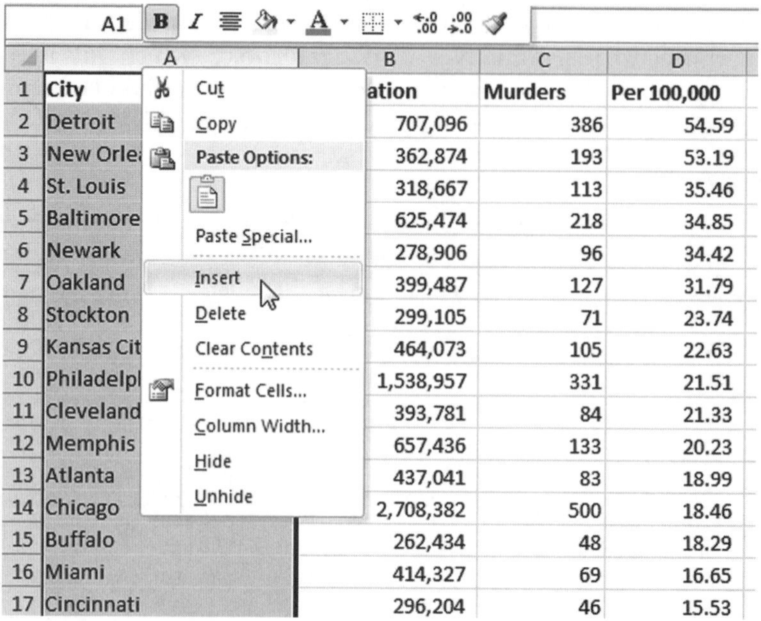

By clicking on "Insert," you get a new column to the left of the cities as in **Figure 4.9,** and you can type in a column title, "Rank."

Figure 4.9

	A1	▼ ⬤ ✕ ✓ ƒx	Rank		
◢	A	B	C	D	E
1	Rank	City	Population	Murders	Per 100,000
2		Detroit	707,096	386	54.59
3	⬦	New Orleans	362,874	193	53.19
4		St. Louis	318,667	113	35.46
5		Baltimore	625,474	218	34.85
6		Newark	278,906	96	34.42
7		Oakland	399,487	127	31.79
8		Stockton	299,105	71	23.74
9		Kansas City	464,073	105	22.63
10		Philadelphia	1,538,957	331	21.51
11		Cleveland	393,781	84	21.33

Now type "1" in A2 and "2" in A3, as shown in **Figure 4.10.**

Figure 4.10

	A3	▼ ⬤ ✕ ✓ ƒx	2		
◢	A	B	C	D	E
1	Rank	City	Population	Murders	Per 100,000
2	1	Detroit	707,096	386	54.59
3	2	New Orleans	362,874	193	53.19
4		St. Louis	318,667	113	35.46
5		Baltimore	625,474	218	34.85
6		Newark	278,906	96	34.42
7		Oakland	399,487	127	31.79
8		Stockton	299,105	71	23.74
9		Kansas City	464,073	105	22.63
10		Philadelphia	1,538,957	331	21.51
11		Cleveland	393,781	84	21.33

Highlight both A2 and A3, and place the cursor in the lower right-hand corner of A3 so that you see the narrow cross as in **Figure 4.11**.

Figure 4.11

	A	B	C	D	E
	A2		fx	1	
1	Rank	City	Population	Murders	Per 100,000
2	1	Detroit	707,096	386	54.59
3	2	New Orleans	362,874	193	53.19
4		St. Louis	318,667	113	35.46
5		Baltimore	625,474	218	34.85
6		Newark	278,906	96	34.42
7		Oakland	399,487	127	31.79
8		Stockton	299,105	71	23.74
9		Kansas City	464,073	105	22.63
10		Philadelphia	1,538,957	331	21.51
11		Cleveland	393,781	84	21.33

Double-click on the narrow cross, and you will have a ranking for each city, as shown in **Figure 4.12**. This allows you to provide readers or viewers with an idea of how their city compares to other cities in terms of murders.

Figure 4.12

	A	B	C	D	E
1	Rank	City	Population	Murders	Per 100,000
2	1	Detroit	707,096	386	54.59
3	2	New Orleans	362,874	193	53.19
4	3	St. Louis	318,667	113	35.46
5	4	Baltimore	625,474	218	34.85
6	5	Newark	278,906	96	34.42
7	6	Oakland	399,487	127	31.79
8	7	Stockton	299,105	71	23.74
9	8	Kansas City	464,073	105	22.63
10	9	Philadelphia	1,538,957	331	21.51
11	10	Cleveland	393,781	84	21.33

Filtering

After creating rates and ranks for all the cities, you might want to compare only the largest cities. Without creating a new worksheet, you can use the Filter function of the spreadsheet. That is, you can filter in or filter out the data you want depending on the criteria, just as you would in a Google Advanced Search.

Go to the toolbar and click on "Data," as you did when you wanted to sort. Except this time, choose "Filter" and click on it, as shown in **Figure 4.13**. (You must have at least one cell in the worksheet highlighted.)

Figure 4.13

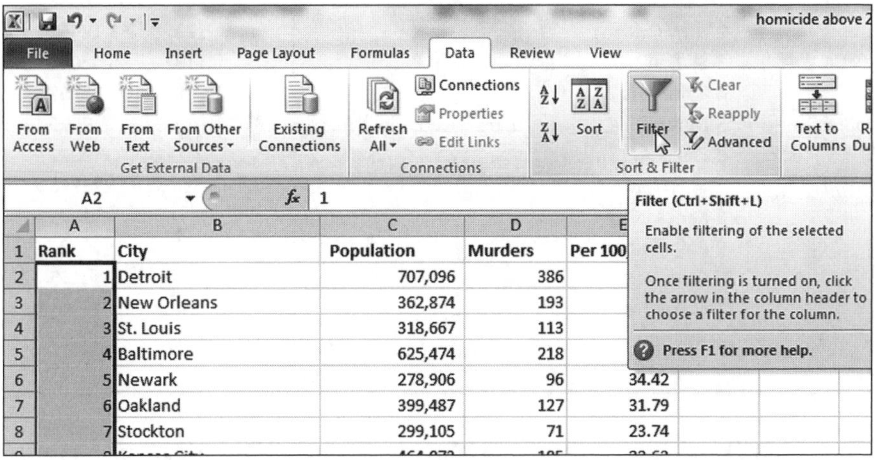

By clicking on "Filter," you create small scroll arrows for each column, as shown in **Figure 4.14**. Place the cursor on the scroll arrow next to "Population."

Figure 4.14

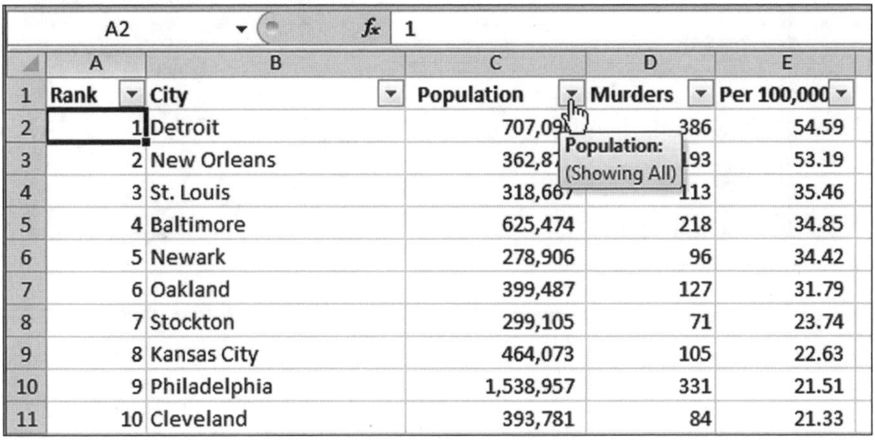

Click on that arrow and then click on "Number Filters" and choose how you will filter the worksheet; for instance, as "Greater Than Or Equal To," as shown in **Figure 4.15**.

Figure 4.15

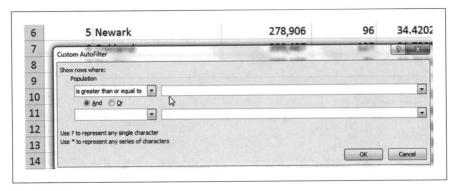

Click on the arrow next to "Greater Than Or Equal To," as in **Figure 4.16**, and you will get a box to place a number in.

Figure 4.16

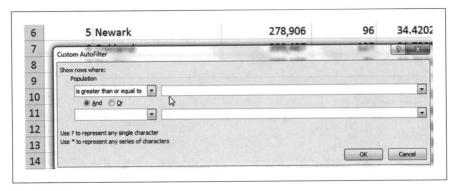

Now, type "1000000" (1 million), as in **Figure 4.17**. (Note that this box uses Boolean logic—and, or, not—mentioned in Chapter 2, which allows you to employ more specific criteria.) This kind of filtering of information based on a criterion will be discussed again in Chapters 5 and 6, on database managers. In database software, filtering is known as choosing the criteria or using a where statement.

Figure 4.17

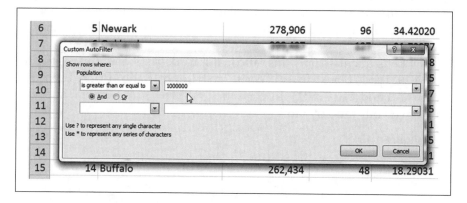

Click "OK." You now will have a much smaller set of data comparing cities with populations of 1,000,000 persons or more. Note that Chicago in now in second place and New York is in ninth place, as shown in **Figure 4.18**.

Figure 4.18

	A2	▾	f_x	1		
	A	B		C	D	E
1	Rank ▾	City ▾		Population ▾	Murders ▾	Per 100,000 ▾
10	9	Philadelphia		1,538,957	331	21.51
14	13	Chicago		2,708,382	500	18.46
24	23	Dallas		1,241,549	154	12.40
31	30	Houston		2,177,273	217	9.97
39	38	Phoenix		1,485,509	123	8.28
41	40	Los Angeles		3,855,122	299	7.76
47	46	San Antonio		1,380,123	89	6.45
52	51	Las Vegas Metropolitan Pc		1,479,393	76	5.14
55	54	New York		8,289,415	419	5.05
68	67	San Diego		1,338,477	47	3.51

Ratios

A ratio is another powerful calculation to make comparisons that can be more understandable. For example, a ratio can provide one number that can show the difference in the chances of being in an accident, getting a disease, or receiving a grant.

Journalists looking into home mortgage loans have used ratios to illuminate the disparity in loans made by banks to whites and to minorities. If 30 percent of black applicants for loans are denied loans and 10 percent of whites are denied loans, a ratio comes in handy.

Let's calculate only this ratio in a spreadsheets, as shown in **Figure 4.19**. Type "Black" in A1, "White" in B2, and "Ratio" in C2. Type "30" in A3 and "10" in B3. In C3, type "=A3/B3," hit "Enter," and you have your ratio of 3 to 1.

Figure 4.19

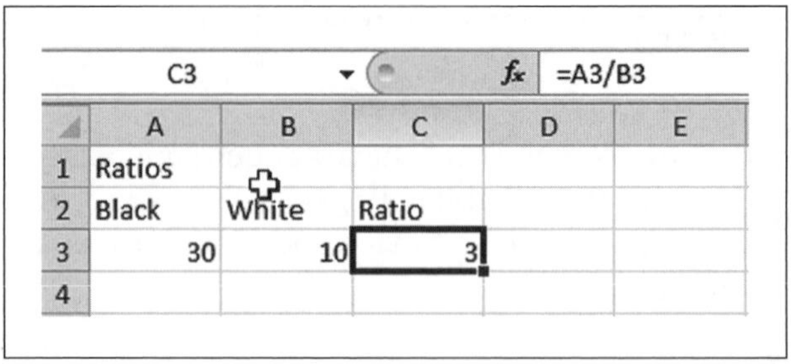

Now, you can convey the disparity more simply by saying that three times as many blacks as whites are denied loans.

Rich Gordon, a journalism professor at Northwestern University, shared a classic example of the use of ratios when he worked at *The Miami Herald* in the 1990s: The sheriff in Broward County, Florida, said he wanted to go after illegal drug dealers as opposed to arresting those who only possessed the drugs. Gordon obtained data on drug arrests of both dealers and users in counties in Florida so that he could see if the sheriff was actually focusing on dealers and also how the sheriff compared to other county sheriffs. Column C shows the total arrests for sales, and Column D shows the total arrests for possession (see **Figure 4.20**).

Figure 4.20

	A	B	C	
1	COUNTY	POP	TOTAL SAL	
2	FLORIDA	13,091,952	20,56	
3	ALACHUA	183,773	105	520
4	BAKER	18,905	29	37
5	BAY	128,575	261	386
6	BRADFORD	22,749	18	86
7	BREVARD	409,370	396	1,372
8	BROWARD	1,278,384	2,700	6,687
9	CALHOUN	11,216	21	0
10	CHARLOTTE	11,557	85	123
11	CITRUS	95,915	48	76

You can find the user/dealer arrest ratio by dividing the number of those arrested for possession by those arrested for dealing drugs, D2/C2, and hitting "Enter" to get your answer, as shown in **Figure 4.21**.

Figure 4.21

=D2/C2

	A	B	C	D	E
1	COUNTY	POP	TOTALSALE	TOT_POSS	RATIO
2	FLORIDA	13,091,952	20,566	42,506	2.066809
3	ALACHUA	183,773	105	520	
4	BAKER	18,905	29	37	
5	BAY	128,575	261	386	
6	BRADFORD	22,749	18	86	

To get rid of all but two decimal places, click on the comma in the toolbar. (In some cases, you might not want any figures after the decimals.) By sorting the data in descending order—based on ratios— Gordon found the sheriff had not distinguished himself in any major way from sheriffs in other counties (see **Figure 4.22**).

ure 4.22

BROWARD

	A	B	C	D	E
1	COUNTY	POP	TOTALSALE	TOT_POSS	RATIO
2	ALACHUA	183,773	105	520	4.95
3	LEON	198,269	153	734	4.80
4	BRADFORD	22,749	18	86	4.78
5	ST. JOHNS	86,118	50	213	4.26
6	MARTIN	103,083	95	381	4.01
7	NASSAU	44,957	13	51	3.92
8	BREVARD	409,370	396	1,372	3.46
9	VOLUSIA	376,695	509	1,754	3.45
10	PALM BEACH	883,044	808	2,557	3.16
11	SARASOTA	279,577	284	889	3.13
12	PINELLAS	855,763	1,061	2,998	2.83
13	BROWARD	1,278,384	2,700	6,687	2.48
14	POLK	414,700	511	1,179	2.31
15	DADE	1,961,694	3,907	9,014	2.31
16	GLADES	7,922	11	24	2.18
17	FLORIDA	13,091,952	20,566	42,506	2.07

For a further look at the sheriff's performance, you could also obtain a rate of possession arrests per 10,000 persons. You would use 10,000 as a multiplier because of the population range of the counties. Divide the number of possession arrests by population—and multiply by 10,000. If you copy the formula and then sort based on Column F, you will see in **Figure 4.23** that the Broward County sheriff's arrest rate of those who are caught possessing, not selling, drugs is among the highest in the state.

Figure 4.23

BROWARD

	A	B	C	D	E	F
1	COUNTY	POP	TOTALSALE	TOT_POSS	RATIO	RATE
2	CHARLOTTE	11,557	85	123	1.45	106.43
3	MONROE	79,536	389	427	1.10	53.69
4	BROWARD	1,278,384	2,700	6,687	2.48	52.31
5	VOLUSIA	376,695	509	1,754	3.45	46.56
6	DADE	1,961,694	3,907	9,014	2.31	45.95
7	COLUMBIA	43,534	114	186	1.63	42.73
8	BRADFORD	22,749	18	86	4.78	37.80
9	LEON	198,269	153	734	4.80	37.02
10	MARTIN	103,083	95	381	4.01	36.96

Pivot Tables

We have used "Sum" to total columns of numbers, but often we also need Summarize data. By that we mean that we need to do a subtotal of numbers by each group within a data set. For example, you might need to summarize the total cost of employee salaries in each agency of a department.

In another example, you might be adding up all the salaries of twenty-five players on each of twenty teams. That means that you would take a total of 500 rows of information and reduce them to twenty rows of subtotals.

Often, in looking at campaign financial records, journalists want to sum up how much each contributor gave to candidates, or how much each candidate collected in contributions. To do this in a spreadsheet, use a "pivot table" because it allows you to get all those subtotals in one overall calculation. Let's say we have a list of political contributors, as shown in **Figure 4.24**.

Figure 4.24

	A	B	C	D	E	F	G
1	LAST	REST	ZIP	OCCUPATION	CONT_DATE	AMOUNT	CAND_ID
2	GRUBB	KITTY	37920	ATTORNEY	10/5/2011	1000	H0TN02017
3	DUNCAN	RICHARD	37919	ATTORNEY	11/23/2011	200	H0TN02017
4	NORTON	FRANKLIN	37901	ATTORNEY	11/2/2011	200	H0TN02017
5	WHELCHEL	BARBARA	37922	HOUSEWIFE	9/28/2011	1000	H0TN02017
6	WHELCHEL	WARD	37939	ATTORNEY	9/28/2011	1000	H0TN02017
7	SHIPLEY	ROBERT	37917	MACHINIST	11/2/2011	200	H0TN02017
8	HARDING	SAMUEL Y	37919	CLOTHING DIST	9/15/2011	200	H0TN02017
9	FURROW	SAM	37901	FURROW AUCTION	7/22/2011	500	H2GA08038
10	GENTRY	MACK A	37901	CENTRY AND TIPTO	8/23/2011	250	H2GA08038
11	CONLEY	WILLIAM M	37915	REGAL GROUP	2/25/2011	1000	H2TN03052
12	WARDLEY	J A	37922	SELF/NOVA INC	3/29/2011	1000	H2TN06014
13	MILLIGAN	JAMES	37902	ATTORNEY	8/5/2011	1000	H2TN07038

We see that we have contributors' last name, first and middle name or initial, ZIP code, where they are from, their occupation, a contribution date, the amount they gave, and the ID of the candidate they gave to. (We will make good use of the Candidate ID in the database manager discussions in chapters 5 and 6.)

We might want to find out how each contributor gave to a candidate, how much each occupation contributed, or how much came from each ZIP code. A pivot table will allow us to do perform these calculations. To use a pivot table, first go to "Insert" on the menu bar and click on "Pivot Tables," as in **Figure 4.25**.

Figure 4.25

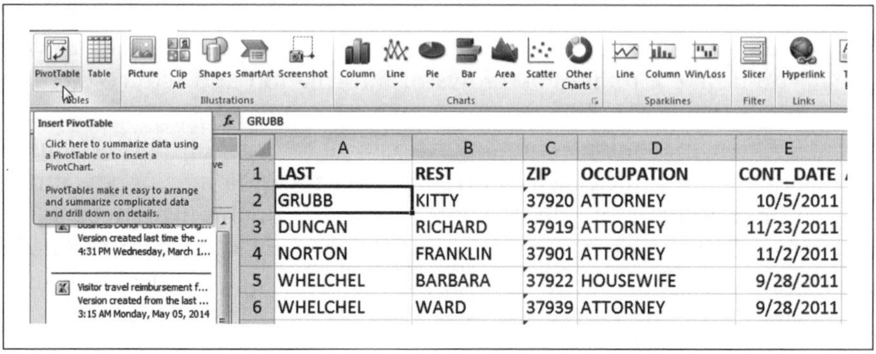

You want to make sure you have a cell highlighted in the worksheet when you click on "Pivot Table." That means Excel will automatically choose the range of all your data. It should be $A$1 (including the header row) through $G$542. (See **Figure 4.26**.)

Figure 4.26

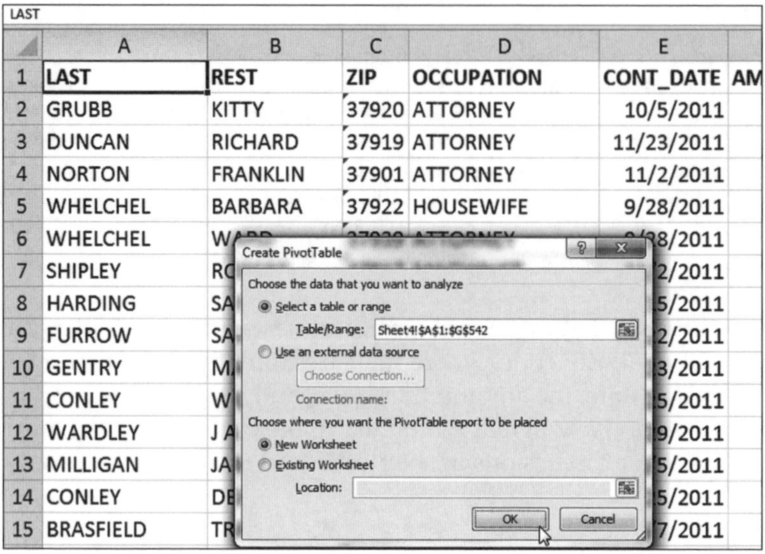

Click on "OK" and the next screen is the template for the pivot table as seen in **Figure 4.27**. You may want to take a minute or two to get oriented. On the right side, you can see that you have the names of your columns in the upper window and that the lower window has places to do calculations. On the left side, you have the area where you can "build" your pivot table. (For purposes of illustration, the right side and left side have been moved closer together, something you can do yourself.)

Figure 4.27

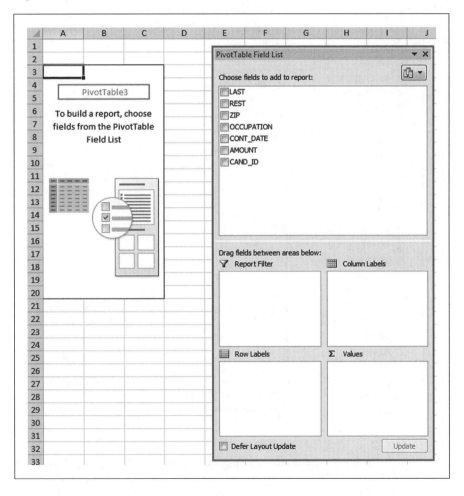

For your first summary of data, click on "LAST" in the right-hand box. You will notice that "LAST" now appears in the right-hand box under "Row Labels." On the left side is a column containing every unique last name (see **Figure 4.28**).

Figure 4.28

If you were to scroll down, you would see that 541 rows have crunched into 285 rows of names because there are many rows with the same last name. To see the total given by each of the persons with the same last name you should click on the box next to "AMOUNT" in the upper right-hand box. You will see that "Sum of AMOUNT" appears in the lower right-hand box under "Values." On the left side, you have a second column called "Sum of AMOUNT" with a total given by each person with the same last name (see **Figure 4.29**).

Figure 4.29

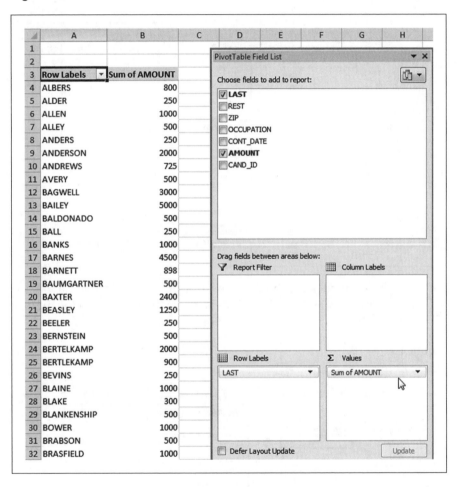

To sort the Sum of AMOUNT, highlight the first record in the second column, which reads 800, click on "Data" in the menu bar, and then click on "Z to A," which means the data will be sorted from the highest to lowest amount (see **Figure 4.30**).

Figure 4.30

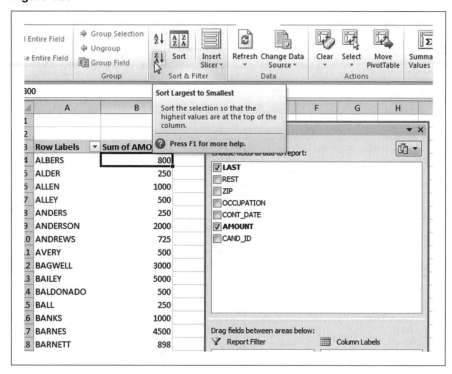

After you click on the "Z to A" button, you will now have your data sorted, and you will see that the name "Haslam" and the highest total, 29500, rise to the top. (See **Figure 4.31**.)

Figure 4.31

	A	B	C	D	E	F	G	H
1								
2				PivotTable Field List			▾ ✕	
3	Row Labels	Sum of AMOUNT		Choose fields to add to report:				
4	HASLAM	29500	✛					
5	WOOD	17750		☑ **LAST**				
6	CONLEY	9500		☐ REST				
7	LEE	6010		☐ ZIP				
8	GOODFRIEND	6000		☐ OCCUPATION				
9	TALBOTT	5500		☐ CONT_DATE				
10	CLAYTON	5250		☑ **AMOUNT**				
11	BAILEY	5000		☐ CAND_ID				
12	COLEMAN	4500						
13	BARNES	4500						
14	LOVE	4250						
15	HARRISON	4150						

If you want to count the number of contributions rather than the amount, you can click on "Sum of AMOUNT" in the lower right-hand side and click on "Value Field Settings," as in **Figure 4.32**.

Figure 4.32

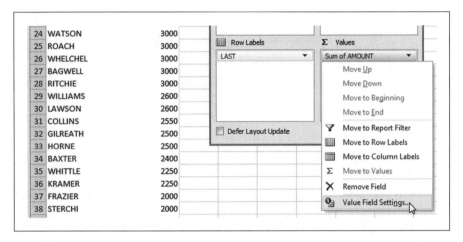

You will get a choice of calculations. You should pick "Count," as shown in **Figure 4.33**.

Figure 4.33

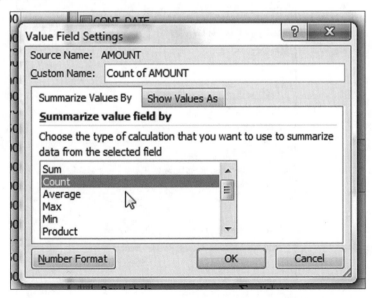

When you click on "Count," the data in the Sum of AMOUNT column will change the number of donations (see **Figure 4.34**).

Figure 4.34

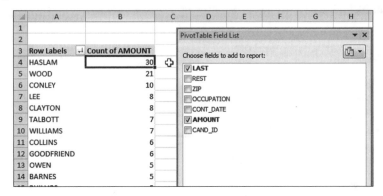

If you want both a column of the sum of amounts and a column of the count of donations, you can drag AMOUNT to the lower box so that you have two AMOUNTs. The second one will default to Sum of AMOUNT and add the third column to your pivot table, as in **Figure 4.35a** and **4.35b**.

Figure 4.35a

Figure 4.35b

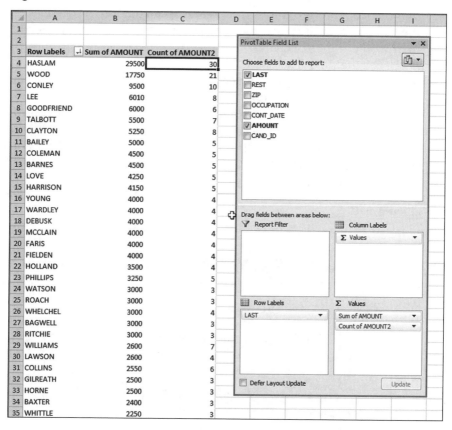

There are many other kinds of analyses you can do with a pivot table, but this gives you an idea of its potential.

Pivot tables also are good preparation for working with database manager software. With each tool, you are grouping similar kinds of information together and totaling the amount. In a database manager, which handles many more records in an easier fashion, this is known as the "Group By" function. In a database manager, you would Group By NAME in the previous example and "Sum" the amounts.

Charts and Graphs

There is one last activity to do that can make all the difference in spreadsheets: visually displaying the results of your analysis graphically. By using visualizations, you see differences instantly and don't have to slog through columns and rows of calculations. Spreadsheets permit you to easily place information into bar charts, pie charts, and many other kinds of charts.

Using the data discussed above, you could chart the data set of cronies to see which employee received the highest percentages, clearly illustrating this information in a bar chart.

First, highlight the Name column. Then, holding down the control key, move the cursor to the Percent (of raises) column and highlight that column. Then click on "Insert" in the upper toolbar and click on the icon of a bar chart called "Column." You will see that you can pick from different types of bar charts, as shown in **Figure 4.36**.

Figure 4.36

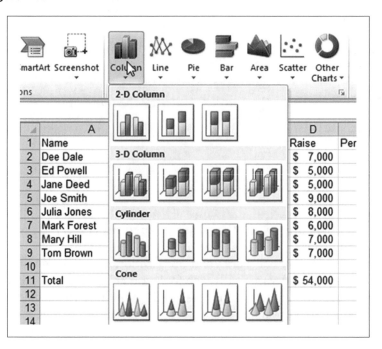

Go ahead and pick the "2-D Column." You will instantly get a bar chart showing the differences in the percentage of raises the cronies received (see **Figure 4.37**). Furthermore, it is a chart that you can enlarge, move around, or copy and paste. (Note that you can save the chart in its own worksheet.)

Figure 4.37

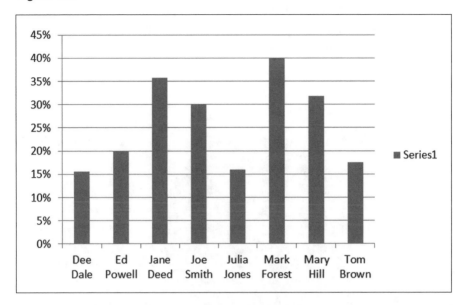

You can similarly display increases in crime with a bar chart or easily represent a budget with a pie chart. Sometimes, doing this helps you see the results of your work more clearly. For example, residents of a city may believe they are paying too much for sewer and water services. They claim that commercial businesses use more water and put a burden on the sewer system but don't pay their fair share. You could obtain the budget figures for revenue from the division and put them on a spreadsheet, as shown in **Figure 4.38**.

Figure 4.38

	A	B
1	Water and sewer division	This year
2		
3	Residential water fees	$ 18,405,222
4	Residential sewer fees	$ 8,324,555
5	Commercial water fees	$ 11,504,302
6	Commercial sewer fees	$ 5,662,131
7	Investment interest	$ 1,445,214
8		
9	Total	$ 45,341,424

You can format these figures in a pie chart by choosing that graphic. This will show what kind of percentage and proportion the amounts have, as in **Figure 4.39**, and make it clear whether the residents may have a legitimate complaint.

Figure 4.39

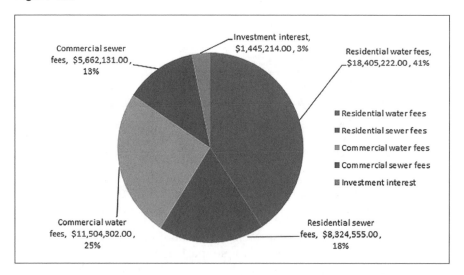

As you can see, spreadsheets can provide detailed analysis and comparisons as well as vivid graphics that make it easier to understand the results. After some practice with spreadsheets, you will be ready to move to database managers, where some of the same analyses can be done, but much more quickly and with many more records. Most important, files (known as tables in database managers) can be joined and columns from different files can be used to create a new database.

CAR Wars

During the past decade, West Virginia education officials closed one of every five schools in a massive consolidation drive. Parents and opponents said rural children were forced to ride the bus four hours a day or longer. State officials said most children rode the bus for only a short time.

We started with asking a simple question: "How long are children's bus rides in West Virginia?" When we looked for electronic records we found that most school districts in 35 rural counties did not keep computerized records. So we obtained the paper records from the counties and built our own database in Excel that included when each run started, when it stopped, and how much time spent in between. Excel was the right tool because we were doing calculations involving the differences in time.

We found the number of children who rode the bus more than two hours a day had doubled. Also, we found that two-thirds of the bus routes carrying elementary schoolchildren exceeded the state guidelines that said children should not be on a bus longer than an hour a day.

The state transportation director promised to computerize all records and conduct his own study.

—Scott Fine and Eric Eyre, *The Charleston Gazette*

Chapter Checklist

- The use of rates and ratios is a way to fairly compare entities with different populations.
- Spreadsheets allow you to narrow your analysis by filtering the information you want to use.
- Pivot tables give you a way to total information by categories.
- Charts allow you to clearly visualize information and effectively present your findings.

Your Turn to Practice

1. Find the FBI Website and download information in a worksheet on crime by year throughout the United States.
2. Open the file in Excel and calculate the crime rates, using the number of crimes and the populations, for violent crimes and for property crimes.
3. Do a ratio of property crimes each year to violent crimes each year.
4. Create a pie chart of property crimes and violent crimes from the most recent year.
5. Download campaign finance information from the Center for Responsive Politics.
6. Use a pivot table to illustrate which party received the most funds.

Database Managers, Part 1

Searching and Summarizing

> *A team of reporters and editors began culling and analyzing state data from nearly 30,000 crashes over five years along Florida's 382 miles of I-95. In an initial 10-page report, we delivered the news that the number of people killed on the Florida highway had doubled over five years.*
>
> —Tony Manolatos, *Florida Today*

> *Just how big is the legal gambling industry in Ohio and in the nation, we wondered, and what impact have casinos, multi-state lotteries and other forms of betting in neighboring states had on Ohio? The Ohio Lottery Commission provided an electronic database of sales from stores that sold lottery tickets for the past several years. That made it fairly easy to analyze sales by ZIP codes with Microsoft Access. Using that database and other statistics, The Dispatch was able to estimate that a large chunk of $9.9 billion in revenue from Ohioans' gambling went to neighboring states.*
>
> —Barnet D. Wolf, *The Columbus Dispatch*, Ohio

Both of these stories involved large databases and many categories of information that a spreadsheet might handle, though not as easily as a database manager. If your data comes in a relational database, which contains two or more tables (files of information), a database manager is an absolute necessity.

The overall value of learning to use a database manager is that it can examine hundreds of thousands of records efficiently, organize them into similar groups, and compare the records in one table with the records in one or more other tables. Some reporters use a database manager to do what they call the "heavy lifting" of data analysis—that is, searching, summarizing, and matching large databases.

Many U.S. journalists start using a database manager to analyze campaign finance records. These records cross over many topics because they can be used to track contributors' access to elected officials and influence regarding issues such as education, health, business, and environment. You can get these records from public agencies or from nonpartisan, nonprofit groups that make them easy to use. In some instances, journalists create their own databases.

Years ago, journalists conscientiously kept tabs on campaign contributions to politicians. Some kept lists, some kept index cards, and some kept the information in their head. But with the advent of databases, most journalists began to download the data and analyze it in a spreadsheet or database manager.

A journalist should learn to use a database manager as soon as possible for two technical reasons. A spreadsheet is not made to handle hundreds of thousands of records in different files that need to be matched. In addition, governments often keep data in relational databases, which contain two or more files that have to be joined. So you need to know how to use a database manager in order to analyze that kind of data.

Don't be overwhelmed by database managers, and don't be overwhelmed by the design of the database in **Figure 5.1**. This is not a database that a journalist just beginning to work with data would start out with, but it does show why you need a database manager. A spreadsheet is not designed to handle different tables joined together by information known as key fields.

The following schema—that is, diagram—in **Figure 5.1** shows how different files on the transportation of hazardous materials can be joined and related to each other through common information: "IDs."

Figure 5.1

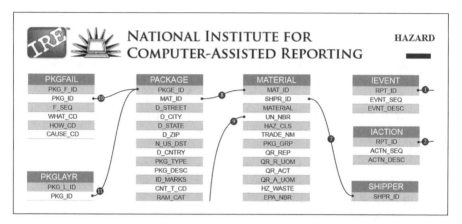

The Federal Election Commission (FEC) in Washington, D.C., maintains this kind of relational database on campaign finance information regarding contributions to federal candidates and to political committees. In the United States, you can also obtain this information online from nonprofit groups such as the Center for Responsive Politics (www.opensecrets.org) or the National Institute on Money in State Politics (www.followthemoney.org).

By using databases to monitor campaign donations and expenditures, journalists can come up with a good selection of story ideas; they also can readily see how data analysis can lead to a story. Furthermore, many editors support doing stories on this particular topic because most consider it required public service to monitor campaign finance and explain how it influences governmental actions and business.

In addition, a campaign finance database can be used for longer analytical stories while serving as an instant resource for daily stories. After an election ends, a reporter can do a story on how much money the winner received and from whom the winner received it. Then, after the winner takes office and begins to award no-bid contracts, the reporter, using a database manager, can quickly link the recipients of generous contracts to campaign contributors. A typical headline may read: "Mayor's Supporters Get Lucrative Contracts."

Another reason campaign contributions are good fodder for learning how to use database managers is because you initially have to concentrate on only a few columns of information (see **Figure 5.2**).

Figure 5.2

| Contributor | Contribution | Candidate |

For purposes of this chapter and Chapter 6, we will use a somewhat modified version of real data. We have chosen a classic database used for teaching over the years because it not only is from the federal election database, it also contains many of the shortcomings common to databases. This specific database contains information on campaign contributions to congressional candidates in Knoxville, Tennessee. (For simplicity, the version in this chapter leaves out two columns, city and state.) To see the data in Microsoft Access, we open the program and then open the database called campaignfinance, as in **Figure 5.3**.

Figure 5.3

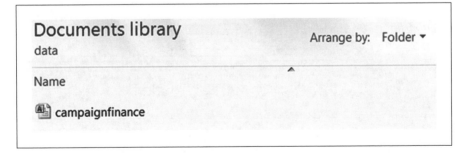

Documents library
data

Arrange by: Folder ▾

Name

campaignfinance

When you click on "campaignfinance," the database will be opened in Access, as in **Figure 5.4.**

Figure 5.4

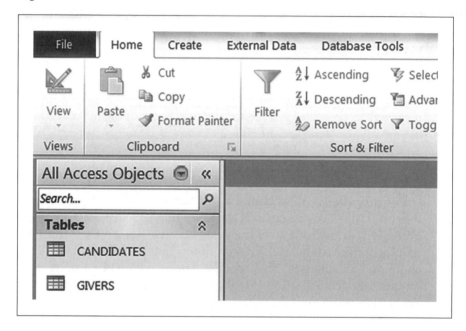

Notice that there are two files known as Tables. This means that a database in Access is like a folder. It can contain one or more tables, often intended to be used together. Click on "CANDIDATES," and you will see the data in the table, as in **Figure 5.5.**

Figure 5.5

ID	NAME	PARTY1	ADDRESS1	CITY	STATE	ZIP	DISTRICT
H0TN02017	DUNAWAY, DAVID H	DEM	100 S FIFTH STREET	LA FOLLETTE	TN	37766	04
H2GA08038	CHAMBLISS, C SAXBY	REP	PO BOX 190	MOULTRIE	CA	31776	08
H2TN03052	WAMP, ZACHARY P	REP	4705 N FOREST ROAD	HIXSON	TN	37343	03
H2TN06014	SUNDQUIST, DONALD K	REP	3028 EMERALD STREET	MEMPHIS	TN	38115	07

It looks much like a spreadsheet, but the field names (columns are known as fields in database managers) are embedded. Database managers are meant to be used by more than one person, so the software makes it a little difficult to change column names or the layout of the data.

Notice that you no longer have letters and numbers to guide you. One difference between spreadsheets and database managers is that information in spreadsheets usually comes to you in some sort of order. In database managers, the information initially may be in a random order because the software assumes you will reorder the information constantly, according to your needs. Furthermore, database manager programs aren't set up to copy formulas, which is why spreadsheets have addresses of numbers and letters.

After reviewing the field names and data, close the table by hitting the "x" in the upper-right-hand corner of the screen and open the "GIVERS" table, as in **Figure 5.6.**

Figure 5.6

LAST	REST	CITY	STATE	ZIP	OCCUPATION	AMOUNT	CAND_ID
GRUBB	KITTY	KNOXVILLE	TN	37920	ATTORNEY	1000	H0TN02017
DUNCAN	RICHARD	KNOXVILLE	TN	37919	ATTORNEY	200	H0TN02017
NORTON	FRANKLIN	KNOXVILLE	TN	37901	ATTORNEY	200	H0TN02017
WHELCHEL	BARBARA	KNOXVILLE	TN	37922	HOUSEWIFE	1000	H0TN02017
WHELCHEL	WARD	KNOXVILLE	TN	37939	ATTORNEY	1000	H0TN02017

These are the contributors who gave to the thirty-one candidates in the CANDIDATES table. There are 541 contributors listed, so this is just a sample from that election. But it is enough to work with and learn about *queries* of the data that could be applied to any database.

The two tables are meant to be joined by a *key field*. In this case, the key field is CAND_ID in the GIVERS table and is the ID number that is given to the candidate by the FEC. In the CANDIDATES table, the field that has the candidate ID numbers is called ID.

You may ask why the data was not all placed in one table. Putting the data in two tables saved time because the candidate information had to be typed only thirty-one times (for each of the thirty-one candidates) as opposed to 541 times (the number required for each contribution record). This approach also efficiently stores the data about the same topic in one table—that is, all the givers are in one table and all the candidates are in another. We will start our analysis, however, by examining only one table, GIVERS.

The Query

Unlike working with a spreadsheet, when using a database, you do not do your work directly with the original data. Instead, in a somewhat more formal procedure, the database manager has you create a query in a different screen and then has you *run* the query to create a new and temporary table, or data set.

A fairly easy way to do this is through use of a query design. Close the GIVERS table, click on "Create" in the tool bar, and then go to "Query Design," as shown in **Figure 5.7**.

Figure 5.7

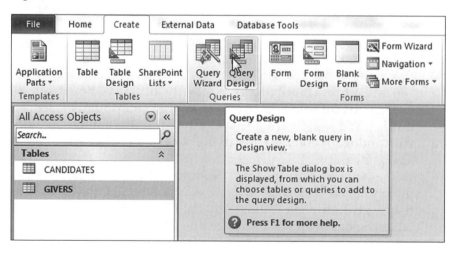

Click on "Query Design." You get a choice of the two tables to examine, as in **Figure 5.8**.

Figure 5.8

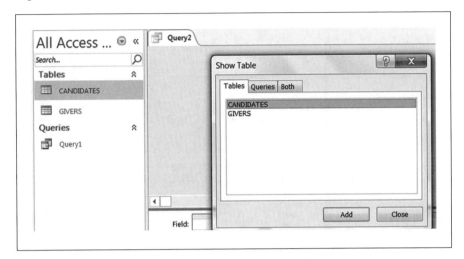

Move the cursor to "GIVERS" and click on "Add"; the table's field names will appear in a box in the upper window. This is the table you want to analyze, so close the lower box from where you added the tables, as shown in **Figure 5.9**.

Figure 5.9

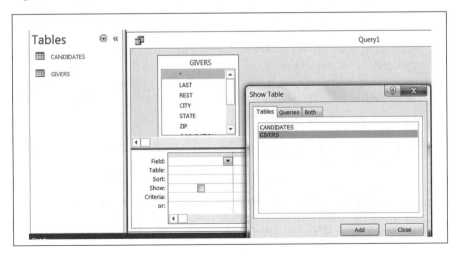

After you close the lower box, you are ready to build your query in **Figure 5.10**.

Figure 5.10

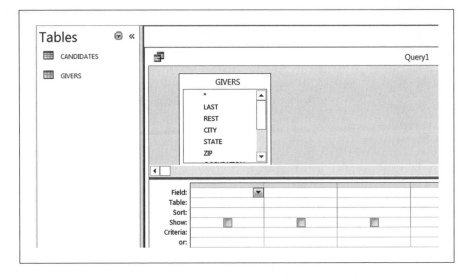

Selecting and Searching

A key strength of a database manager is speedy searches. If you want to find a name and the information related to it, you tell the database manager that you want to look for all the information on that particular name.

First, you select the columns you want to use. The concept of select allows you to cull through the columns in a database. (Often, government databases have thirty or more columns of information.) Selection of the fields is important because it clears away distractions. Furthermore, many journalists' analyses eventually involve only four to six fields to enable them to focus on subsets of information.

In **Figure 5.11**, you need to select only three fields—REST, LAST, AMOUNT—to see who gave how much. (REST is first and middle name, if any, and LAST is last name.) You do this by double-clicking on each field name in the upstairs window. The field name appears in successive columns in the downstairs screen. (You can also drag the field names to the columns in the downstairs window.)

Figure 5.11

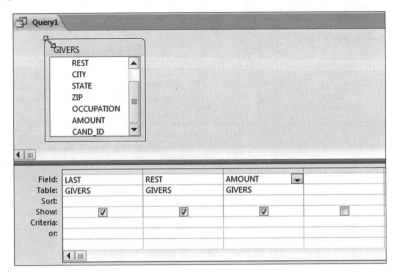

Make sure that a check mark appears in the box on the "Show" line so that the information in that field will appear in the answer. Now, go to the menu bar and click on the exclamation mark (!) to run the query, as shown in **Figure 5.12**.

Figure 5.12

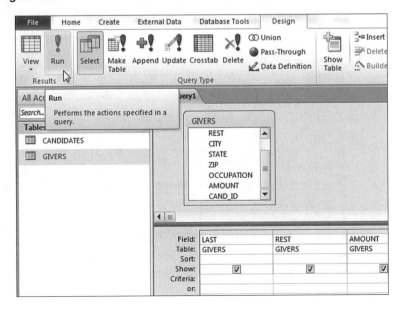

As a result of this query, we get only the three fields we chose, as shown in **Figure 5.13**.

Figure 5.13

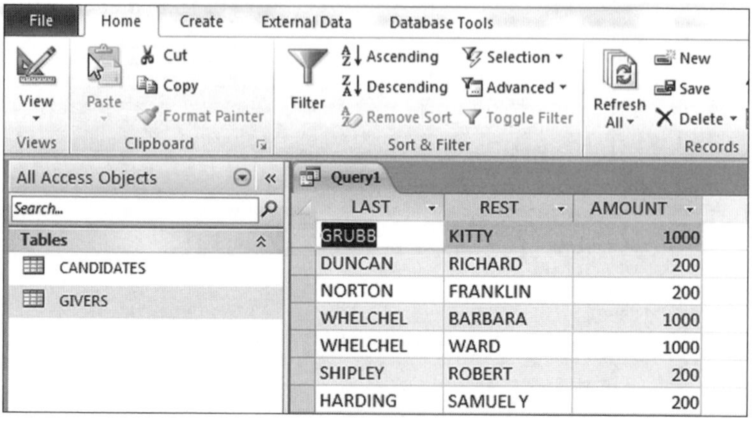

We have not lost any of the other information in the "GIVERS" table, but have simply selected three fields temporarily to show in our answer. This "vertical" cut of the information, that is, choosing fields (columns), shows us how easy it is to include some information and exclude other information. If we don't save this result, it will simply disappear when we return to the original information.

To return to our query form, we just hit the "View" symbol in the left-hand top corner, as in **Figure 5.14**.

Figure 5.14

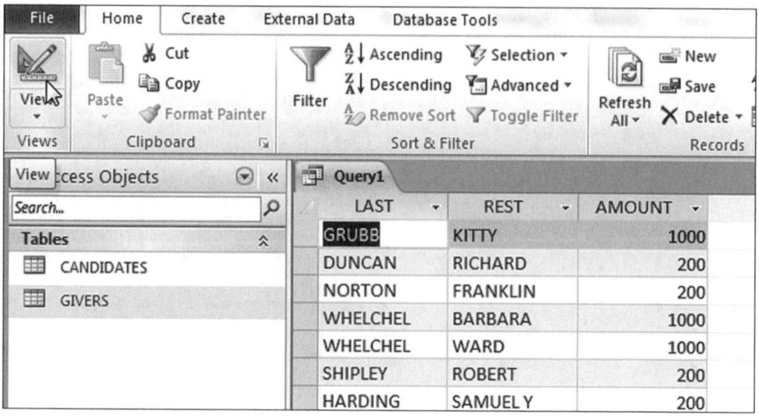

Criteria and Filtering

After looking at the fields, you might want to look just at the contributors who gave more than $500. The concept is the same as what we explored in Chapter 4, where you used the filter in Excel to limit the information you received.

After returning to your query form, click on the criteria box in the downstairs window under "Amount" and type "> 500," as shown in **Figure 5.15**.

Figure 5.15

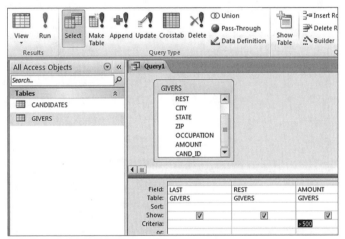

Now, run the query, and your answer appears as in **Figure 5.16**, showing only those who gave more than $500. (A helpful hint: When you type a number such as 1000, do not put in any commas or the program may not read it correctly.)

Figure 5.16

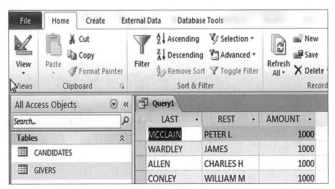

Sorting

If you want to sort the contributions from highest to lowest, you use the same principle as in the spreadsheet. Click the icon to return to the query form, choose the amount field, and identify the sorting order as "Descending," as shown in **Figure 5.17**.

Figure 5.17

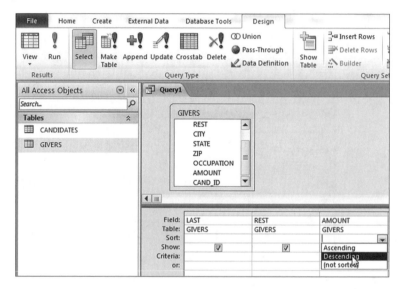

After you run the query, you will see that the answer is now sorted by highest amount to lowest, as in **Figure 5.18**.

Figure 5.18

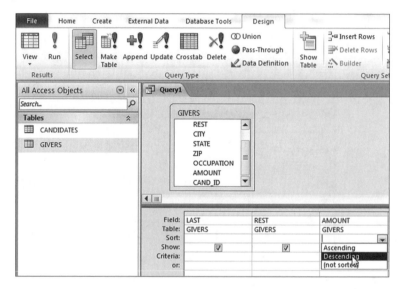

Criteria and Wildcards

Database managers allow you to single out one individual by using filters. The filters may be under "Criteria" or they may be in "where" statements (which we will cover later), such as: where Last = "Haslam"

Database managers also have another powerful filtering function called *like*. This function lets you choose a name using only a few letters of the name. Because data entry can be an error-prone endeavor, names are often spelled in several different ways in governmental databases. Using *like* is one way to get around the problems.

As shown in **Figure 5.19**, you can look for all the Haslams by using *like* and something known as a wildcard. (By the way, get rid of >500 in the criteria line so that you will see all contributions by the Haslams.)

In the Access database manager, the wildcard is an asterisk (*). Just as a joker in a deck of cards can stand for anything, the wildcard after "HASL*" stands for all the numbers or letters that might follow the letters "HASL." (Lowercase or uppercase doesn't matter.)

In **Figure 5.19**, you type in "HASL*" under the LAST field, hit "Enter," and the word "Like" is automatically entered. Then, run the query.

Figure 5.19

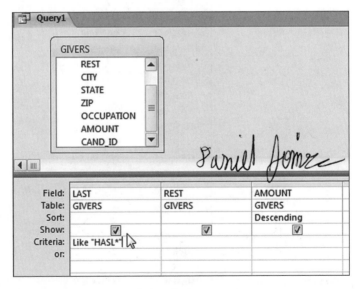

Your query result picks up every name that begins with "HASL." If a data-entry error was made, such as Haslam incorrectly being entered as "Haslem," then using "HASL*" ensures that you do not miss any of the misspelled entries (see **Figure 5.20**).

Figure 5.20

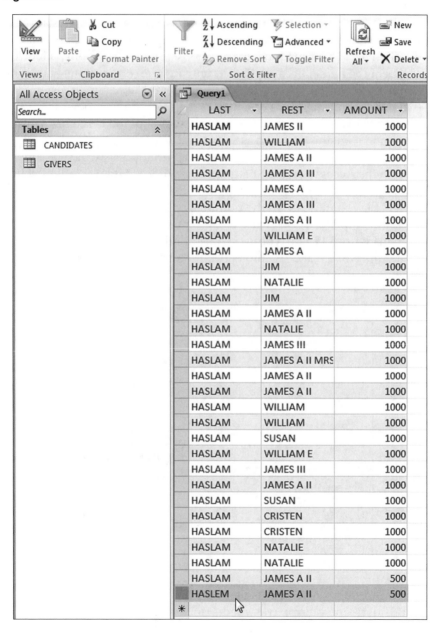

Boolean Logic: And, Or, Not

Another strength of database managers is that the search can incorporate two or more criteria easily in a query. To do that, you use the logic we spoke about in Chapter 2—Boolean logic. Some modern librarians call it a "life skill." It also is a routine way of doing online searches. Boolean logic uses the words *and*, *or*, and *not*. Those three little words are incredibly powerful.

You might want to search for everyone who is an attorney or surgeon who gave more than $500 to a candidate. Boolean logic treats the search in this way: give me everyone who donated who is a surgeon *or* an attorney *and* who gave more than $500.

Access and other user-friendly database managers actually are making it easy to do Boolean logic. In most searches online, or in more sophisticated databases, you would write: where (occupation = "surgeon" or "attorney") and amount > 500. (We will address this kind of language in Chapter 6.)

You have to pay attention to your use of *or* and *and*; also be very careful with *not*. If you are choosing items in the same field, don't write: where city = "New York" *and* city = "Los Angeles." How can you be in two places at once?

Also as a general rule, if you are choosing items in the same field, you should put parentheses around them. For example, if you are looking for all the murderers in New York City *or* Los Angeles, you would write: city = ("New York" *or* "Los Angeles") *and* crime = "murderers." Note that you would probably get all the criminals in New York City and all the murderers in Los Angeles if you instead write: city = "New York" *or* city = "Los Angeles" *and* crime = "murderers."

Not is particularly handy when you want to exclude a set of information. If you are analyzing an election in Wisconsin and you want to look at only out-of-state contributors, you would use a not. Your query would specify the exclusion: where state = *not* "Wisconsin."

Let's return to our table on the presidential contributions and look for every attorney or surgeon who gave more than $500. As shown in **Figure 5.21**, we will delete the current fields in the bottom window and then double-click on "LAST," "OCCUPATION," and "AMOUNT" to add them to the downstairs window.

Under OCCUPATION, we will type "surgeon" or "attorney" on the criteria line. Under AMOUNT, we will type ">500."

Figure 5.21

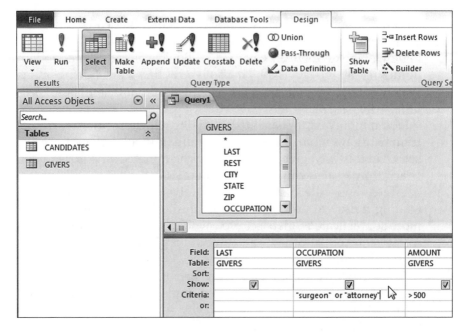

This translates to wanting to see the name of everyone whose occupation is attorney or surgeon and gave more than $500. If we run
the query, we get the results shown in **Figure 5.22**.

Figure 5.22

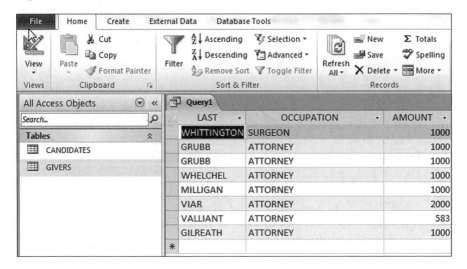

Grouping

Once you have selected your fields, set your criteria, and sorted the data, you still might want to know which occupation gave the most money. This is where the idea of grouping or, as it's known in database parlance, "Group By" comes in.

Group By is the way to quickly summarize data to look for patterns, trends, outliers, and even errors in the data. This is one of the sharpest tools that a journalist can use in a database manager. It accomplishes the same goal as pivot tables in spreadsheets, but once learned it can be more efficient.

First, we decide what category (field) we want to Group By and what field we want to add up. In this example, we want to total the amount for each OCCUPATION. We start a new query in our query form by clearing the downstairs window. To do this, move the cursor to the bar just above the fields into the thin bar until you get a downward-pointing arrow and then dragging the arrow across the columns that you want to clear, thus darkening them. Then hit "Delete," as in **Figure 5.23**.

Figure 5.23

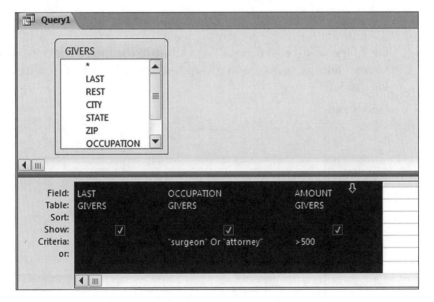

Now we double click on "OCCUPATION" and on "AMOUNT" in the top window to start our new query, as shown in **Figure 5.24**.

Figure 5.24

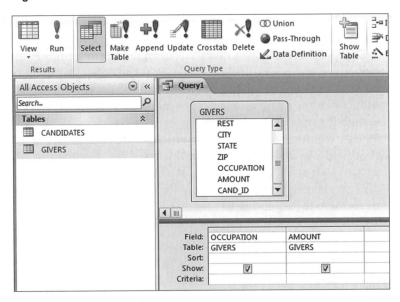

We will use the AMOUNT field to total the contributions. To total the amount for each occupation, we will have to hit the "Total" button in the menu bar; this will add a line to the lower window where we can tell the software to group and total the contributions, as in **Figure 5.25**.

Figure 5.25

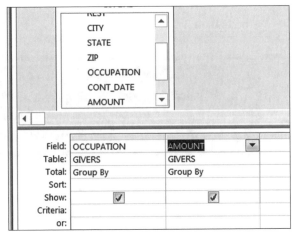

After clicking on "Total," we will see the new line called "Total" in the lower screen, as in **Figure 5.25**. Note how "Group By" shows up on that line under the two fields.

We want to Group By the occupation, that is, divide up the contributions for each occupation. But we don't want to group the amounts; we want to Sum them as we did when we were using pivot tables in Chapter 4. So we click on the arrow next to "Group By" under AMOUNT and select "Sum," as shown in **Figure 5.26**.

Figure 5.26

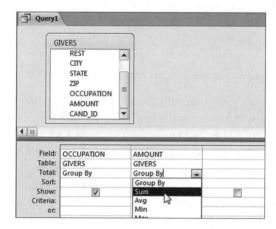

After choosing "Sum," we also can choose to sort our results in descending order by the total amounts so that we will see which candidate received the most money (see **Figure 5.27**).

Figure 5.27

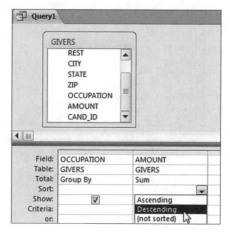

Run the query, and there is your answer, totaling contributions by occupation, sorted highest to lowest (see **Figure 5.28**).

Figure 5.28

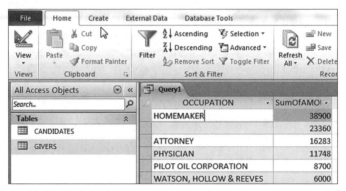

Your query can actually raise further questions to ask. Why is home-maker the biggest contributing occupation? Why is the second-biggest not identified? Is anything being done to make those contributors disclose their occupation? And who runs Pilot Oil Corporation?

You also can count the total number of contributions by using Group By. It's a bit trickier because the best way to count items in a table is to type "Count(*)" in the field name and choose "Expression" instead of "Group By," as shown in **Figure 5.29**. By using this method, you will count not only the fields filled in, but also the blank fields. The database manager does not automatically count blanks fields, so the blanks will not be counted unless you enter "Count(*)," as in **Figure 5.29**.

Figure 5.29

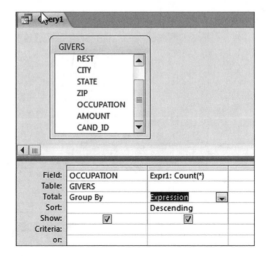

After you type in "Count(*)" and choose "Expression," make sure you are still sorting in descending order. When you run the query, you will get a count of the total number of contributions made to each candidate—both by contributors who identified their profession and those who have a blank for occupation, as in **Figure 5.30**.

Figure 5.30

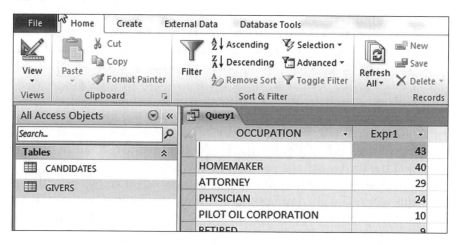

By running this query, you can see that most contributors do not disclose their occupation (or the campaigns do not disclose it).

Once you feel comfortable with these different queries, you will be able to take advantage of this highly effective method of data analysis, which has been the basis for many computer-assisted reporting stories. You obtain information, divide the information into groups, count or sum parts of the information by groups, and sort your results from highest to lowest. (In the midst of the query, you may filter in or filter out information based on other criteria, such as where statements.)

Once you know the formula, you can effectively analyze many different kinds of information. You could look at a prison population, divide it into races, and then count the number to find the percentage of minorities versus whites in prison. You could then compare these figures to the percentage of minorities in the community.

You could look at blighted properties in your city, divide the information into neighborhoods, and then count the number of blighted properties in each neighborhood. You could take thousands of records of federal contracts in your state, divide the information by communities in which work is being done, sum the amounts of the contracts, and get an idea of the economic importance of federal contracts to those communities. You could look at records of toxic chemical emissions into the environment by manufacturers, divide the information by the communities where the manufacturers are located, sum the emissions by communities, and then find out which community has the most toxic releases.

Much of the information you collect can be examined in this way. With this base information in hand, you can start the traditional reporting process—including interviews and site visits—at an advanced level. With analyses of the relevant databases, you already will know about trends and patterns, will have considered the impact of anomalies (the "outliers"), and are already thinking of follow-up questions. It is as though a tipster or an inside source called you on the phone and told you what you should be investigating. Except that the tipster is not a person, it's database.

In the next chapter, we will look at more advanced ways of doing this work. The upcoming skills will show you how to compare tables to come up with unique stories and will give you even more control in analyzing data.

CAR Wars

Compared to other states, Georgia may still struggle to shore up weak public school academic records, but schools and taxpayers spare little expense to field competitive football teams.

Teaming with David Milliron, the newspaper's director of computer-assisted reporting, we built a comprehensive database of the nearly 2,400 high school football coaches and assistant coaches in the state. The database was built in Microsoft Excel and analyzed in Microsoft Access.

Gathering the salary and teaching assignment information from 312 public schools proved to be a daily battle. Initially, districts refused to comply or said it would cost hundreds of dollars to produce the information, but eventually we got the data for the salaries for teachers and coaches. By having the database, we were able to group and total salaries and search quickly for individual information.

Once we had done our analysis and our reporting, we published stories questioning whether education is being compromised for playing football games. We found nearly $80 million in state tax dollars spent for coaches' salaries in one year; and head football coaches making 55 percent more than the average for academic teachers.

—Mike Fish, *The Atlanta Journal-Constitution*

Chapter Checklist

- Database managers handle large numbers of records and allow you to organize the data the way you want.
- Database managers can do speedy searches for particular information and catch typos in data incorrectly entered—the key is using wildcards.
- Database managers allow you to filter information easily.
- Database managers can quickly create summary data by grouping categories of information and allowing you to total the numbers or items in those groups.

Your Turn to Practice

1. Get a database of registered gun dealers in your state from the U.S. Bureau of Alcohol, Tobacco, Firearms and Explosives from the bureau's Website (www.atf.gov) or from this book's Website (www.ire.org/carbook/).
2. Query the database, searching for your city.
3. Perform a query in which you group and count the gun dealers in each city in your state. Sort the records by the cities with the highest to lowest number of gun dealers.
4. Write another query in which you group and count the gun dealers by ZIP code in your city. Sort the records from highest to lowest number of gun dealers.

Database Managers, Part 2

Matchmaking and Advanced Queries

Taking two large databases, one of people licensed to work as aides in home health care and one of criminals, The Star-Ledger, based in Newark, New Jersey, found more than 100 recently convicted criminals certified to work unsupervised in the homes of the most vulnerable residents of the state. The matching of criminal identities with aides' identities helped reveal lax state policies and also helped protect those needing assistance at home.

—Robert Gebeloff, *The Star-Ledger*

As you can see from this public-service story, one of most valuable uses of a database manager is matching information in one file to information in another file.

This chapter covers *relational databases,* in which files known as tables are intentionally joined to one another. Information is separated into *linked* tables because it organizes the information and cuts back on the amount of time it takes to do data entry and analysis. But many reporters also use database managers to perform enterprising comparisons of files never created to be linked together—as Robert Gebeloff, now at *The New York Times,* did in cross-referencing files of licensed health-care providers and recently convicted criminals in the example above.

For decades, reporters have looked at relationships between people and organizations. In campaign finance, they have tracked businesses' contributions to a candidate and government contracts that those businesses were awarded after the candidate won election.

Other reporters have looked at criminal incidents in the context of local police department decisions on deploying patrol officers. Others examined environmental agency files on waste dumps and their locations and then looked at U.S. Census information to see whether the dumps were being placed in low-income areas, where the local populace had little political clout.

Relational Databases

Utilizing a database manager and relational databases to do these tasks—once done with hard-copy records—is the way this traditional kind of reporting is now typically performed.

In the twenty-first century, information about you is kept in many relational databases. (That's how marketing people find you to make those annoying phone calls, send you spam e-mails, or barrage you with direct mail.)

If you have a job at a large business or with a government agency, the organization probably manages your paycheck in a relational database. **Figure 6.1** illustrates what the record layout in a table that includes your information might look like.

Figure 6.1

Employee	
Field Name	Data Type
EmployeeID	Text
Lastname	Text
Firstname	Text
Street	Text
City	Text
ZIP	Text

In another table is a list of the paychecks you received and the date that you received them. **Figure 6.2** shows the record layout in this table.

Figure 6.2

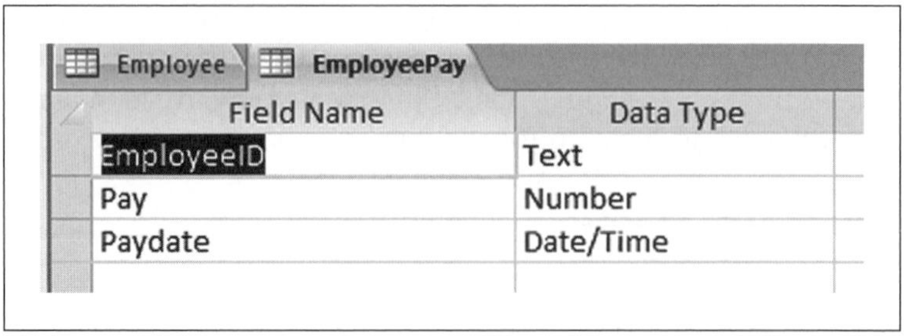

Note that each table has an employee ID and that only an ID, not a name, appears in the paychecks table. The ID field is known as a key field. It's the field that links the two tables together.

In a relational database, you link tables together using a query that links the key fields. By linking the two tables, an employee's name with payroll information is matched to his or her mailing address. This data structure saves space and time because you don't have to type address information about the employee with each entry about payroll. The tables also organize information efficiently into subjects. And database managers can automatically create key fields of IDs or can use an already existing ID.

What's the most universal key field in the United States? The Social Security number. If you have someone's Social Security number, you can link tables and tables of information together from different databases.

Joining Tables

But how do you create such a link? You tell the database manager that when the ID number in a record in the employee table equals the ID number in employee payroll, then the information should be matched, creating a new record potentially with all the columns of information in both tables. In Access, you can actually draw a line from one table to another by clicking on the employee ID field and then dragging the cursor onto the employee ID in the salary table as in **Figure 6.3**.

Figure 6.3

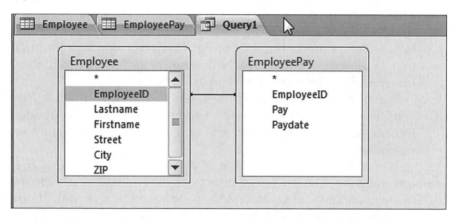

In other database managers, the software automatically guesses the connection for you. You can also write a *where* statement in a universal programming language known as Structured Query Language (SQL). The statement would link the two files together (as in **Figure 6.3** where the Employee ID in the Employee table = the Employee ID in the Employee Pay table).

Later in this chapter, we will write some basic SQL statements because SQL is a straightforward programming language that every good database manager has for analysis. In addition, SQL helps you think clearly about the questions you are asking and ask them quickly, once SQL is mastered.

Many governmental databases you ask for will be relational, as shown in Chapter 5. You need to know what government officials mean when they say it's a relational database. You also need to know to ask what the key field is.

As you learned in Chapter 5, one of the most used databases in the United States is from the Federal Election Commission (FEC). If you obtain data from the FEC, you will receive a candidates table, a political action committee contribution table, an individual contributor table, and a political committee table. You can link those tables by the ID numbers of committees and candidates.

To find information about a candidate, you would go to the candidates table. In that table, you would find ID numbers for the committees set up by the candidate to receive and record contributions. To find information about the committees, you would link the candidates table to the political action committee contribution table through the ID numbers. To determine which individuals contributed to the candidate, you would link the committee table to the individual contributor table, again using the committee ID that is present in both tables. It's not unlike building bridges between islands of information, as shown in Chapter 5 in the diagram of the hazardous material transportation database and its tables.

For our immediate purposes, we can look at the slightly simplified FEC data we used in Chapter 5. One table contained information on contributors, and one contained information on candidates.

To use the two tables in a query, click on the "Create a Query" button and go to "Design View." Instead of just adding one table to the upstairs window, add both tables, one at a time, as shown in **Figure 6.4**. Note that the candidate table, CANDIDATES, has been added, and now we are adding the contributors in GIVERS.

Figure 6.4

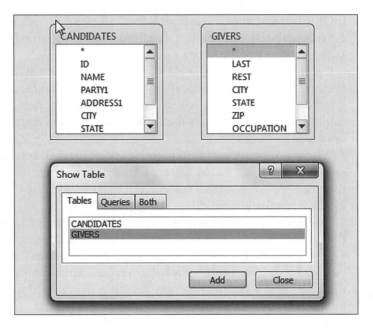

After adding both tables, we click our cursor on "ID" in CANDI-DATES and drag it to "CAND_ID" in GIVERS to link the tables (see **Figure 6.5**).

Figure 6.5

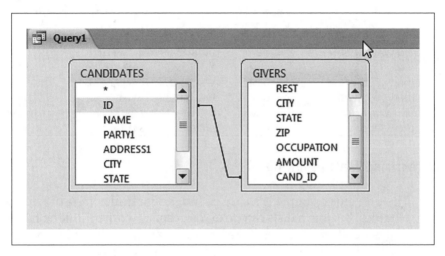

Now that we have correctly linked the tables, we can treat the two tables as one and choose fields from each as though we were at one big buffet table, as shown in **Figure 6.6**.

Figure 6.6

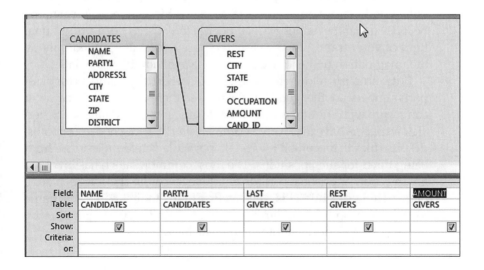

Run the query, and you will get the fields from both tables, as in **Figure 6.7**.

Figure 6.7

NAME	PARTY1	LAST	REST	AMOUNT
DUNAWAY, DAVID H	DEM	GRUBB	KITTY	1000
DUNAWAY, DAVID H	DEM	DUNCAN	RICHARD	200
DUNAWAY, DAVID H	DEM	NORTON	FRANKLIN	200
DUNAWAY, DAVID H	DEM	WHELCHEL	BARBARA	1000
DUNAWAY, DAVID H	DEM	WHELCHEL	WARD	1000
DUNAWAY, DAVID H	DEM	SHIPLEY	ROBERT	200
DUNAWAY, DAVID H	DEM	HARDING	SAMUEL Y	200

Enterprise Matchmaking

The previous example is a case of "intentional" matching or joining of tables. But journalists can do extraordinary work by linking tables that weren't created to be linked. In this way, journalists can cross the borders between agencies, professions, and fiefdoms.

For more than two decades, journalists have used enterprising matching to ferret out criminals in school systems, nursing homes, or home health-care programs. Other examples include finding out if lottery sales are primarily in low-income areas and if legislators who set taxes are actually paying their own. Journalists seeking information on dead voters voting have linked street addresses or names of voters with names on death certificates. (Why seek this information? Because using the names of dead people to vote has been a traditional kind of voter fraud.) In any case, the possibilities are limited only by the imagination of the journalist and the availability of the data.

But journalists seldom have others' Social Security numbers (or passport numbers, another good form of ID) and therefore must be creative in coming up with one or more key fields to link unrelated databases. Several newspapers have discovered criminals working in school classrooms, despite rules that prohibit felons—in particular, child molesters—from being hired for such positions. The most common match has involved linking court or prison records to employee records. This has been done by matching several fields, such as first name to first name, last name to last name, and date of birth to date of birth (if you can get it) or by linking other identifying information such as addresses.

In **Figure 6.8**, for example, you have teachers. (None of these names represent real people.)

Figure 6.8

Lastname	Firstname	DateofBirth	DateofHire	School
Smith	Joseph	11/1/1965	1/10/1990	Nixon
Barry	Donald	10/12/1955	8/3/1991	Kennedy
Neff	Arnold	4/2/1959	8/3/1991	Jefferson
Harwood	Mary	3/14/1969	8/3/1991	Jefferson
Atwater	Gerald	2/1/1953	9/5/1991	Madison

In **Figure 6.9**, you have a table of criminals.

Figure 6.9

Lastname	Firstname	DateofBirth	Charge
Barry	Donald	10/12/1955	Child Molest
Smith	Walter	2/14/1957	Child Molest
Walker	Edward	5/10/1961	Child Molest
Nadell	Samuel	12/4/1962	Rape
Harwood	Mary	3/14/1969	Assault

Since you don't have a key field, such as a Social Security number, you look at both tables and choose several fields. To link, you click and drag each similar field (see **Figure 6.10**).

Figure 6.10

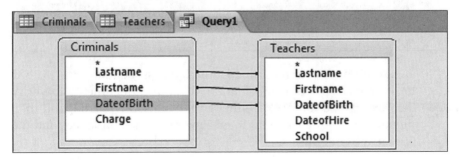

In this case, select the fields Lastname, Firstname, School, and DateofBirth from the Teachers table, and DateofBirth and Charge from the Criminals table to display, as shown in the bottom window in **Figure 6.11**.

Figure 6.11

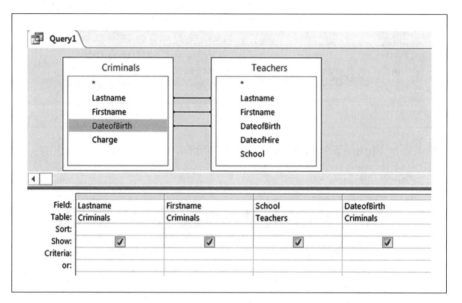

Run the query, and the result would look like **Figure 6.12**, showing the potential matches between teachers and criminals.

Figure 6.12

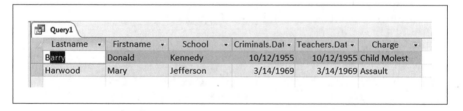

At this point, your reporting would have just begun. You will need to double-check your information, use other documents to verify that any record matches are indeed for the same person, and then prepare to conduct difficult interviews with the employees and the school system officials.

A good number of *matches* (or *hits*, as they are sometimes known) in such unrelated databases can lead to good public-service journalism that protects the weak or vulnerable. *The Charlotte Observer* in North Carolina produced such a story. In Massachusetts, Brad Goldstein at *The Eagle-Tribune* found welfare recipients in jail by matching the names of recipients with a list of prison inmates. At *The Miami Herald* in Florida, Steve Doig matched building inspection records after Hurricane Andrew with wind velocities in the same areas; if the wind velocity was low and the damage was high, then he knew there likely was a problem with construction standards in that area. Reporters at *The Atlanta Journal-Constitution* in Georgia discovered that teachers who were convicted felons had escaped scrutiny when being hired. Other reporters have compared parking tickets and weather conditions to show that such tickets are seldom given out when the weather is bad.

It should be noted that the value of matchmaking is limited by the validity of the comparison. You need to be sure of the accuracy of each match, and that requires more work. That may mean also finding ways—through other documents and interviews—to confirm that the matches are accurate and your story is solid.

Structured Query Language

Once you have mastered the basics of using the visual *query by example* tool of database managers, you are ready to learn the basics of SQL, the common programming language for doing analysis in most database managers. The name may sound imposing, but many working journalists believe that SQL gives them more flexibility and control over their queries and also makes them think through their analysis more carefully.

SQL has six fundamental commands:

- *Select* is a way of choosing the fields (columns) of information you want. You can also use it to calculate differences in numeric fields or to create new fields.
- *From* chooses which table or tables are used.
- *Where* allows you to filter the records you want to see based on selected criteria.
- *Group By* is a way of summarizing information whenever you perform calculations, such as adding up (summing) amounts or counting the number of times something occurs. Use this command carefully in conjunction with the *select* statement. You generally would not use Group By unless you want to total by categories of information.

- *Having* allows you to limit the number of records in your answer, after you have summarized the records using Group By.
- *Order By* lets you sort your answer from highest to lowest (or vice versa) by a particular field just as you did in a spreadsheet or Access in previous chapters.

To use SQL in Microsoft Access, begin as you did in Chapter 5 when asking questions. Proceed as though you were going to create a new query in the GIVERS table we have been using, and add the table GIVERS, as in **Figure 6.13**.

Figure 6.13

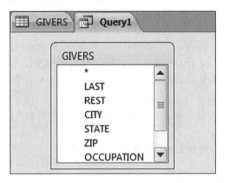

Now, go to the left-hand corner, where the Design View icon is, click on the small arrow next to it, and choose "SQL View," as in **Figure 6.14**.

Figure 6.14

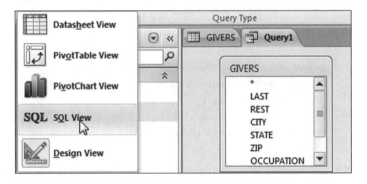

When you click on "SQL View," you are sent to a screen where the program has already started an SQL query for you, as shown in **Figure 6.15**.

Figure 6.15

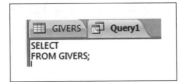

Note that you have SELECT and FROM, which every SQL query must have. Why? Because you cannot ask a question and expect an answer unless you are using a table and choosing the fields that will be included. SELECT says which fields will be chosen, and FROM says which table you will choose those fields from. In this case, you are selecting fields from the table GIVERS. (These examples are given in plain SQL. Access will add more words, which you can erase.)

In this case, let's choose all the fields you want to show, using the asterisk (*) wildcard, as in **Figure 6.16**. (The semicolon at the end tells the program that the line is the end of the query.)

Figure 6.16

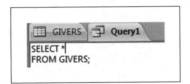

Run the query by clicking on the exclamation mark (!). You get the result in **Figure 6.17** showing the contributors to each candidate and the amount they contributed.

Figure 6.17

LAST	REST	CITY	STATE	ZIP	OCCUPATIO	AMOUNT	CAND_ID
GRUBB	KITTY	KNOXVILLE	TN	37920	ATTORNEY	1000	H0TN02017
DUNCAN	RICHARD	KNOXVILLE	TN	37919	ATTORNEY	200	H0TN02017
NORTON	FRANKLIN	KNOXVILLE	TN	37901	ATTORNEY	200	H0TN02017
WHELCHEL	BARBARA	KNOXVILLE	TN	37922	HOUSEWIFE	1000	H0TN02017
WHELCHEL	WARD	KNOXVILLE	TN	37939	ATTORNEY	1000	H0TN02017
SHIPLEY	ROBERT	KNOXVILLE	TN	37917	MACHINIST	200	H0TN02017
HARDING	SAMUEL Y	KNOXVILLE	TN	37919	CLOTHING DIST	200	H0TN02017
FURROW	SAM	KNOXVILLE	TN	37901	FURROW AUCT	500	H2GA08038
GENTRY	MACK A	KNOXVILLE	TN	37901	CENTRY AND TI	250	H2GA08038
CONLEY	WILLIAM M	KNOXVILLE	TN	37915	REGAL GROUP	1000	H2TN03052

Click on the "Design View" icon and return to "SQL View." This time select just two fields—occupation and amount—in that sequence, as in **Figure 6.18**.

Figure 6.18

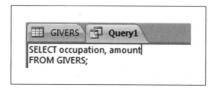

```
GIVERS    Query1
SELECT occupation, amount
FROM GIVERS;
```

Run that query and you see how you can choose just two fields and place them in any order you want to, as in **Figure 6.19**.

Figure 6.19

occupation	amount
ATTORNEY	1000
ATTORNEY	200
ATTORNEY	200
HOUSEWIFE	1000
ATTORNEY	1000
MACHINIST	200
CLOTHING DIST	200
FURROW AUCT	500
CENTRY AND TI	250

GIVERS   Query1

Return to the SQL View. This time, let's use the WHERE statement to limit our result to contributors with the Haslam name (see **Figure 6.20**). Note that we use the word *like* as we did in Chapter 5 and the asterisk wildcard, and we surround the word "HASL*" in double quotation marks. (We have to use quotation marks whenever the field contains text information. *Text* means any combination of letters and numbers.)

Figure 6.20

```
SELECT Last, amount
FROM givers
Where Last like "hasl*"
```

Run the query, and you will see in **Figure 6.21** that you have chosen only contributors with the Haslam name and the one name that is probably a Haslam, but misspelled: Haslem.

Figure 6.21

Last	amount
HASLAM	500
HASLAM	1000
HASLAM	1000
HASLAM	1000
HASLAM	1000
HASLAM	1000
HASLAM	1000
HASLAM	1000
HASLEM	500
HASLAM	1000
HASLAM	1000
HASLAM	1000
HASLAM	1000

Let's return to SQL View and see how easy it is to total how much the Haslams gave. We type in the SELECT statement and type "sum (amount)," just as we did when using Excel. We then put in the WHERE statement with "Hasl*" (see **Figure 6.22**).

Figure 6.22

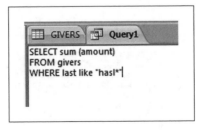

```
SELECT sum (amount)
FROM givers
WHERE last like "hasl*"
```

Run the query. You will see that you get one number, which is the total that all the Haslams gave to each of the candidates, as shown in **Figure 6.23**. The total is given as the field name of an "expression."

Figure 6.23

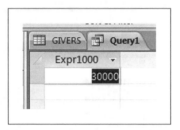

It would be logical to want to see how much each occupation gave, and that is where we use Group By. Remember that Group By divides the records in the table into groups of similar categories so that you can count or sum each group—just like subtotals.

Returning to the SQL View, let's start a new query. We know that we want the occupations; we also want the amount totaled for each occupation. That means that we want two fields in our answer. So we type "SELECT occupation sum (amount)." We know our table is named "GIVERS," so we check to make sure that is what the FROM statement says: "FROM givers."

We are not limiting the contributions to a particular occupation, so we know we don't need a WHERE statement. But we do know we are going to group contributions by occupation, so we type "GROUP BY occupation." We specify a high to low order based on amount with "ORDER BY 2 DESC." Thus, with just a few words, we are finished. Our query should now look like the one in **Figure 6.24**.

Figure 6.24

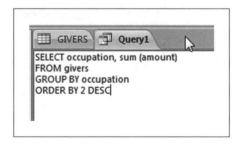

This query is sometimes called the *magic query*. It is the template for summarizing data in large data sets and also for checking the consistency and integrity of the data, as we will show in Chapter 9. Run the query, and you get the total given to each occupation, as in **Figure 6.25**.

Figure 6.25

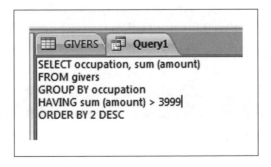

occupation ▾	Expr1001 ▾
HOMEMAKER	38900
	23360
ATTORNEY	16283
PHYSICIAN	11748
PILOT OIL CORf	8700
WATSON, HOLI	6000
RETIRED	5725
COLBAR INC	5000
NOVA INC	5000
WOOD AGENC\	5000
CLAYTON HOM	4750
RITCHIE FELS &	4750

After examining your answer, you may want to limit the number of occupations to include only individuals who gave $4,000 or more. In the query, insert a HAVING statement in your query and type "HAVING sum (amount) > 3999." That means you will get all contributions that are $4,000 or more. HAVING is like the WHERE statement, except that HAVING is only used as a criterion after you have used Group By (see **Figure 6.26**).

Figure 6.26

```
SELECT occupation, sum (amount)
FROM givers
GROUP BY occupation
HAVING sum (amount) > 3999|
ORDER BY 2 DESC
```

When you run this query, the result should look like **Figure 6.27**. As specified, the total contributions stop at $4,000.

Figure 6.27

occupation	Expr1001
HOMEMAKER	38900
	23360
ATTORNEY	16283
PHYSICIAN	11748
PILOT OIL CORF	8700
WATSON, HOLI	6000
RETIRED	5725
COLBAR INC	5000
NOVA INC	5000
WOOD AGENC'	5000
RITCHIE FELS &	4750
CLAYTON HOM	4750
HORNE PROPEI	4500
REGAL CORPOF	4500
WOOD PROPEF	4000
DEROYAL INDU	4000
PILOT CORPOR.	4000

In addition to getting the sum of contributions to each candidate, you can also tell the program to count the number of contributions as shown in **Figure 6.28**. Starting with a fresh SQL query, go to the SELECT statement, add a comma after "sum (amount)," and then type "Count (*)" at the end of the line. Note that you do not really need a space between sum and (amount) or Count and (*). Also note also that Access usually will add "AS Expr1" since, unlike with Sum, it wants to give this Count column a new name.

Figure 6.28

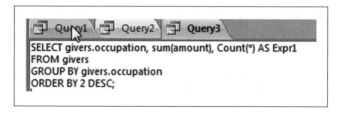

```
SELECT givers.occupation, sum(amount), Count(*) AS Expr1
FROM givers
GROUP BY givers.occupation
ORDER BY 2 DESC;
```

Run the query. As you see in **Figure 6.29**, you can both sum and count at the same time.

Figure 6.29

occupation ▾	Expr1001 ▾	Expr1 ▾
HOMEMAKER	38900	40
	23360	43
ATTORNEY	16283	29
PHYSICIAN	11748	24
PILOT OIL CORF	8700	10
WATSON, HOLI	6000	6
RETIRED	5725	9
COLBAR INC	5000	6
NOVA INC	5000	5
WOOD AGENC\	5000	7
CLAYTON HOM	4750	7
RITCHIE FELS &	4750	8
HORNE PROPEI	4500	5
REGAL CORPOF	4500	5
DEROYAL INDU	4000	4

As previously mentioned, if you need to join tables, SQL also can do that in one step—using the WHERE statement.

For your query design, start by adding the criminal and teacher and then go to SQL View again. You will see that you have the "SELECT FROM Criminals, Teachers" already in place. This time, type "SELECT *" in the first line. You should have "FROM Criminals, Teachers" in the second line. Then type "WHERE criminals.lastname = teachers. lastname and criminals.firstname = teachers.firstname and criminals. dateofbirth = teachers.dateofbirth;" (ending with a semicolon before the close quotation mark) as in **Figure 6.30**.

Figure 6.30

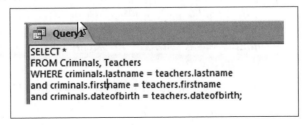

```
Query1
SELECT *
FROM Criminals, Teachers
WHERE criminals.lastname = teachers.lastname
and criminals.firstname = teachers.firstname
and criminals.dateofbirth = teachers.dateofbirth;
```

By running the query, you can see how information from each of the tables was joined to show the outcome of the matches between them, as in **Figure 6.31.**

Figure 6.31

Query1								
Criminals.Las ▾	Criminals.Firs ▾	Criminals.Dat ▾	Charge ▾	Teachers.Las ▾	Teachers.Firs ▾	Teachers.Dat ▾	DateofHire ▾	School
Barry	Donald	10/12/1955	Child Molest	Barry	Donald	10/12/1955	8/3/1991	Kennedy
Harwood	Mary	3/14/1969	Assault	Harwood	Mary	3/14/1969	8/3/1991	Jefferson

SQL is well worth learning. It permits you to perform queries faster, particularly those using Boolean logic. As you have seen, in just a few steps, you have used all of SQL's basic commands, doing far less clicking and dragging than in the visual query by example method. In addition, as you find yourself needing to clean or reshape data, SQL will go far beyond the point-and-click techniques, allowing you to trim out blank spaces, split fields into two, and create programs that will rearrange data.

CAR Wars

The Dayton Daily News *identified 30 cases of neglect by using a database of death cases and a database of group homes for the mentally retarded and documenting drowning of clients, the choking of clients, assaults and other forms of death.*

The overall system of homes for the mentally retarded is cloaked in secrecy and difficult to obtain records from. To get around that, we matched the addresses of 400,000 death records with the addresses of dozens of group homes. Using the matches we found in the addresses, we then contacted family members and examined the inspection records of every group home.

We also talked to group home operators, advocates for the mentally retarded, surviving family members, caseworkers and state and local regulators. Our finding: Ohio's $1.85 billion system to protect 63,000 people with mental retardation is riddled with gaps that have deadly consequences.

As result the governor appointed a task force and the state auditor was asked to audit private companies under contract to provide care.

—John Erickson, *The Dayton Daily News*, Ohio

Chapter Checklist

- Database managers allow you to join two or more tables of information by matching names or identification numbers.
- Not only can you join tables intended to be joined, but you can also join those that no one had thought of joining as a basis for enterprising stories.
- SQL is part of most database managers and is a powerful language that can allow you do many queries more simply and powerfully.

Your Turn to Practice

1. Obtain the relational database called Campaign Finance available at this book's Website (www.ire.org/carbook/). This database has two files: one of campaign donors and one of candidates.
2. Join the tables in the database, as shown in this chapter.
3. Group and sum amounts by last name, by occupation, and then by contribution date. Sort each result by the highest amounts contributed.
4. Repeat the same query using candidate's names.
5. Perform the same queries in SQL.

Part 2

Using Computer-Assisted Reporting in News Stories

7

Getting Data Not on the Web

How to Find and Negotiate for Data

New Jersey state officials turned down the Asbury Park Press' *request that would help the paper measure the performance of the state's child protection agency. But we learned of federal government databases that contained information on children in foster care throughout the United States, including New Jersey. We also learned of a federal law that required the data to be released and used that knowledge to persuade the state officials to release their data for two years.*

We succeeded in getting the electronic information necessary to examine the system and produce a five-day series that showed the state had done little to reform its system and that children were spending more time than ever in foster care and group homes.

—Jason Method, *Asbury Park Press*

Sometimes, the database you need for a story is openly distributed. Sometimes, however, it is kept from you under the guise of confidentiality or national security, even though it would be easy for officials to remove or restrict access to the sensitive material. Officials also may limit access to data by charging absurdly high prices for it. What this means is that a journalist often may have to dig, argue, and push to get data that should be and could be released readily and for free.

This chapter will look at the three steps—finding, negotiating, and importing—for obtaining access to databases so that you can use them in a story. All three steps go together:

1. You need to *find* the right database for the story and determine what information within it you really need.
2. You often need to *negotiate* knowledgeably for the database, avoid stonewalling by bureaucrats who try to snow you with technical terms, and make sure you acquire any supplementary material necessary to understand the database.
3. You need to know how to *import*, or transfer, the data from the source media into the program you intend to use.

When seeking public information in electronic form, remember that taxpayers have already supplied the money to enter the data, store the data, and retrieve the data. Therefore, you should not have to give the agency a good reason to release it. Instead, the keeper of public information should have to give you a good reason *not* to release the information.

In short, you need to think, but not necessarily say: "You have it. I want it. Give it to me." A free and democratic society is based on openness, not bureaucracy and secrecy, and it is a journalist's duty and prerogative to pursue information.

Finding Data

Many journalists starting out in computer-assisted reporting (CAR) wonder where they can find useful databases. The answer is "everywhere."

We will focus on government databases because many private databases not only are hard to get, but also are priced well beyond the budget of a journalist or newsrooms. In addition, many private and commercial databases are actually stitched together from public databases with the very skills you are learning in this book. Quite often, you can do most of the linking of databases yourself.

There are databases on almost any subject and at almost every governmental agency and business. Since the proliferation of personal computers, such organizations have been storing their information electronically. In addition, they have inventoried and indexed their databases more thoroughly than before, an effort that began more than a decade ago, when agencies worried that their databases could be reduced to chaos because of date problems on January 1, 2000.

Even without these guides on a state level or local level, you know that most agencies are computerized and have extensive databases. When you walk into a state office, look around and you'll see everyone typing information into computers. At a city or town hall, you'll see the same thing, whether you are at the building inspector's office or the recorder of deeds', where real estate records are kept.

If you see a report with tables of columns and rows, there generally is a database behind the report, and you should try to get it if it looks useful for your work. For example, state and federal housing agencies often issue reports about where subsidized housing is located, how many units are at that location, and who can qualify for the housing. By asking for the backup electronic information on those reports, a reporter can obtain not only the columns and rows that appear in the reports, but also material that might have been excluded, such as politically embarrassing information.

It's also good to keep in mind that you may be seeing only a portion of a database when you view it on the Web. Often, databases on the Web are only summaries or portions of the original database. It is common for the original database to have information that officials don't want released or don't realize could be of value to the public. And what is on the Web does not always go back for several years.

Although some states require agencies to provide lists of databases, many governmental agencies may say that a database doesn't exist. This may be because they don't want to be burdened with granting requests for data or because they have something to hide.

It is worth investigating whether those same agencies have hired consultants to unravel the mess the agencies made of their computer systems over the past decades. If so, the consultants likely issued reports, and in those reports can be found inventories of hardware, software, and databases—information that can help you determine whether an agency has what you need. To get this information, ask the agency for copies of consultant reports on its computer systems and databases.

Auditors' reports also generally contain an overview of an agency's records and how they are kept. The U.S. Government Accountability Office (GAO; www.gao.gov), a congressional watchdog that performs audits of federal agencies, actually uses many agencies' own databases for its audits. In the back of the GAO reports, the databases are described. Although the databases may not be available online, reports, summaries, and discussions of those databases are mentioned.

You can also look through commercial and governmental database catalogs and online directories. In some cases, an agency staff member may be unaware of the agency's databases. In addition, developing source relationships with social scientists at universities and colleges can open up wide avenues of database possibilities. Those social researchers live in a world of databases, because they rely on data for their statistical analyses.

If you cover a beat, you should develop sources at three levels or more:

1. Talk to data-entry clerks who have little involvement in departmental politics; they can tell you what kind of information they are entering.
2. Talk to data processors; they can tell you what kind of information they are processing.
3. Talk to administrators; they can tell you what kind of information they use for the reports they issue.

In some cases, administrators and their public information officers may not want to talk to the press or may even mislead reporters. That's why it's good to have sources at all three levels. Also, sometimes the administrators and information officers don't even know what databases exist or what they contain.

There are also associations to know about or join. People who belong to groups that use SAS or SPSS (two statistical software packages) know about a wide range of data, from hospitals to insurance to government. The Association of Public Data Users (APDU; http://apdu.org) costs $75 a year to join as an affiliate—but if you can afford it, it's worth it. The APDU puts out a monthly newsletter that discusses various public data.

Obtaining a Database

The first approach to obtaining a database is simply to ask for it. Do not write a formal request under the Freedom of Information Act or your state or country's open records law. Just ask.

In a time of security-conscious officials, you may be required to write a request, but this doesn't happen as often at the local level. But if getting a database becomes cumbersome or the officials demand a formal request, then you will have to hunker down and do some groundwork.

To obtain a database, you need to know what to ask for. You need to know the laws and regulations governing the release of electronic information, though not necessarily to use them as leverage. Sometimes, it is good to know about the rules and regulations so that you *don't* bring them up. Some laws are so antiquated or ambiguous that officials can utilize the laws to effectively block the release of information. To get help on this, check the Reporters Committee for Freedom of the Press (www.rcfp.org) for state laws and the latest on access to databases.

Before you begin to battle for information, make sure you know what database you want and what part of it you must have for the story. Conversely, know what you can give up. If you only really need ZIP codes for your story, don't argue over street addresses.

Finally, you need to know how the information is kept. Is it in a spreadsheet or database manager, or even in some ancient programming language? In what kind of format can the agency give the data to you? What does the record layout look like? How many records are in the file and how large is the file? How many megabytes or gigabytes are in the file? Answers to these questions tell you what hardware, software, and knowledge you will need if you want to make the best use of the data.

The Record Layout

As noted earlier, a record layout tells you the names of the columns, what types of data are in a column (text, numeric, date), and the width of each column. It's your road map to the structure of the database.

If the information is in a spreadsheet, chances are good that you won't need to know too much. With spreadsheets, you generally get the copy and open the file, and your own spreadsheet program automatically places the information on the spreadsheet grid. You will need to know what the names of the columns mean and get a code sheet in case codes are used. You should also check whether the data type is correct and that numeric columns are not mistakenly in text.

Like downloading data from the Internet, that's the easy way to get a database. Frequently, however, you will get information that has been kept in a database manager that you learned about in chapters 5 and 6.

To understand the information in a database, you will definitely need a record layout. A record layout serves as a guide to how the information is stored and ordered. The record layout specifies:

- The name of each field.
- Whether it's a field that is text, also known as alphanumeric or character (consisting of letters and numbers), numeric (only numbers), or dates.
- How wide each field is. A field can contain only so many characters or numbers, depending on its width. (It's like filling out test forms that give you only twelve spaces for your last name. If your last name is Rumpelstiltskin, only "Rumpelstilts" will fit.)
- The position of the field in the record. If a record is 100 characters long and the last name field is the first field and twelve spaces wide, then the last name field's position is one through twelve. Think of a record as a linear crossword puzzle.

Before acquiring a database, you should to get the record layout first. The record layout will tell you what information is in the database and whether it fits your needs. You may need some explanation of the categories of information, because sometimes they are abbreviated with acronyms. For example, you may find the category CANDID. This probably does not mean "candid"; it more likely means "candidate" or "candidate identification number." **Figure 7.1** shows a modified record layout for individual contributors to federal political campaigns.

Figure 7.1

RECIPID	CHARACTER	9
AMENDMENT	CHARACTER	1
REPORT	CHARACTER	3
PRIMGEN	CHARACTER	1
MICROFILM	CHARACTER	11
CONTTYPE	CHARACTER	3
NAME	CHARACTER	50
CITY	CHARACTER	18
ZIP	CHARACTER	5
OCCUPATION	CHARACTER	35
CONTDATE	DATE	8
AMOUNT	NUMERIC	7
OTHERID	CHARACTER	9
COMMCODE	CHARACTER	1
CANDID	CHARACTER	9

As you can see, the field names are somewhat cryptic. You can also see that the record length—if you add up all the fields—is 172 spaces. If each space equals 1 byte of information and you know you are getting 10,000 records, you could calculate how big a file it is. Multiply 172 times 10,000 and you get 1,720,000 bytes, or 1.7 megabytes. In addition, you will need the record layout if you are going to import the information into your own database manager software.

If codes are used in the data but code information is not included in the record layout, you also should obtain the applicable codebook (or code sheet, which means the same thing). This is not programming code, but a document that translates what a code number may actually mean.

Codes are used to save space. Let's say a database maker does not want to write out terms for race and ethnicity, such as "black," "white," or "Hispanic." To save time on data entry and space, the database maker would design the applicable column to have only one character. The database maker then codes blacks as "1," whites as "2," and Hispanics as "3." (Number codes allow statistical software to more easily do analysis.) You might be able to figure that out on your own, but you really don't want to get into a guessing game, as this can result in mistaken assumptions. So obtain the codebook or the code sheet. (Sometimes it also is called a data dictionary.)

You should also get a printout of the first ten to 100 records to see if information has been entered into all of the fields. You also need the printout to make sure that you have transferred the information properly into your computer. Also, get a hard copy of the form from which the information was entered. These are known as integrity checks; we will cover this topic in more detail in Chapter 9.

To review, if you are given a database, you need to ask what language the database is in and request a record layout, a code sheet, and, if possible, a printout of the first 100 records.

Privacy and Security Issues

Over the past decade, politicians and the public have become increasingly concerned about privacy and national security. They have denied requests for electronic information even though the same information is available in hard copy or could be collated from publically available sources.

Jennifer LaFleur, a longtime practitioner and trainer in CAR, was once denied access on an Adopt-A-Highway electronic database. Officials said that, under California law, the information on names in the database was private, even though the names are on public billboards where the donors claim credit for the upkeep of that portion of the highway.

In fact, a group of journalists at a seminar two decades ago came up with thirty-eight excuses that bureaucrats gave for not giving out databases. The same excuses are being used today. You can get the list from the National Institute for Computer-Assisted Reporting (NICAR). Some of those excuses include claims that it will take too much time or the bureaucrat isn't sure how to make a copy of the data.

If an agency claims that its information is private or withheld because of security reasons, you should check the laws and regulations. If the agency is right, you need to decide whether the information you do have access to is still valuable.

Many reporters, by knowing what they need for a story, can agree to the deletion of certain categories. Sometimes you can give up the "name" field because you need the database for a demographic or statistical study. Rather than enter into extended negotiations, consider whether you can give up some fields in exchange for the rest and still get your story.

For instance, reporters often give up names on medical or workers' compensation records because there are a large number of cases in open civil court that can be used for anecdotes. If you are seeking state employee records, you can still do the research for many stories without getting the employees' street addresses.

High Costs

News organizations have been asked to pay millions of dollars when their reporters are seeking information. One time, the database library at NICAR was asked by the U.S. Justice Department to pay more than $2 billion for a database—an absurd amount.

More often, the final cost turns out to be a few hundred dollars or less. Years ago, the state of Connecticut quoted *The Hartford Courant* for a cost of $3 million for access to drivers' license records. Three years later, after extended negotiations, *The Courant* paid a total of $1.

You can prevail on costs if you are willing to haggle and if you know what a fair price should be. Consider the following:

- *The cost of the media.* This should be negligible. A DVD or flash drive costs very little.
- *The cost of copying.* An agency should not charge you for the simple copying of data from a server.
- *The cost of staff time.* Generally, the public has already paid for the collection and storage of data. Unless you ask for special programming, an agency should be hard-pressed to charge you for programming. If it does, the cost should not be more than $20 or $30 an hour.

When possible, you should avoid asking for additional programming. It means that errors can be introduced, and it gives the agency one more chance to remove records that might lead to an embarrassing story. Sometimes, agencies say that creating a special data set is the equivalent of creating *new* records, and some laws do not require an agency to do that.

In practical terms, you should be able to obtain most databases for free or less than $100. Even in those cases where a fee is stated, you should ask for a fee waiver because the Freedom of Information Act generally calls for the waiver of fees if disclosure of the information is in the public's interest.

One threat to the open use of electronic records is the handling of public records by private vendors. Public agencies that don't have computer expertise often hire commercial vendors to do the work for them. But commercial vendors want to make a profit. If a citizen asks for the information, commercial vendors may be allowed by law to charge high costs for copies of the files. Since some agencies don't have a copy of their own records, you then have to argue with the commercial vendor.

Your best solution is to get your news organization and others to push for changing the law. In some states it is illegal for commercial vendors to charge exorbitant prices for public records.

Importing

You don't want to go through all of the work of obtaining a database and then not be able to use it. That's why you have to be careful to get the record layout, size of the file, code sheet, and printout.

There are two key points when you import data. One, make sure that the information goes into the correct columns and that those columns are labeled correctly. Two, make sure that the information is properly translated so that you can read it. This is a much less frequent problem than it used to be.

If you receive the data in one of the common database software programs, your job will be straightforward. It used to be the case that databases created in one software program could not be translated into the database software of other companies, but now most of them can. As an example, if you are importing an Excel file into Microsoft Access, you need only identify the kind of format the database is in, and the information will automatically be loaded into Access. To get to the importing screen, you click on "External Data" under File on the menu bar and click on "Import & Link," as shown in **Figure 7.2**.

Figure 7.2

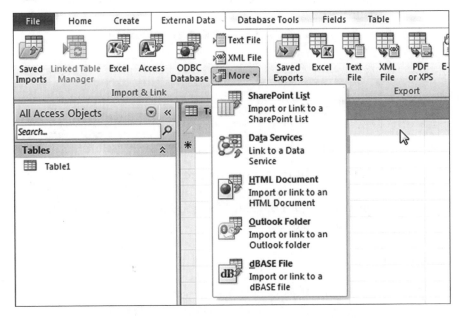

This is very similar to the import screens we see in Microsoft Excel but it is even more extensive. Note that Excel and Access can translate files created with many kinds of software.

Sometimes you will receive information that is *comma delimited* or in *fixed format*, both formats used for databases on the Web. These formats are discussed in Chapter 2.

The comma delimited format is used to save space. Instead of having blank spaces between columns, the columns are shoved together. Programs know to end a column when they see a comma. Quotation marks tell the software that the words in between them should go into character fields. The other information is numeric. (In addition, you often can put field names in the first row to save yourself the time of typing them in again and again.)

Fixed format files are a little tricky because sometimes it is necessary to set up a file to catch the information in the proper column. But Access has a wizard just like Excel, and it will lead you through the same steps (see **Figure 7.3**).

Figure 7.3

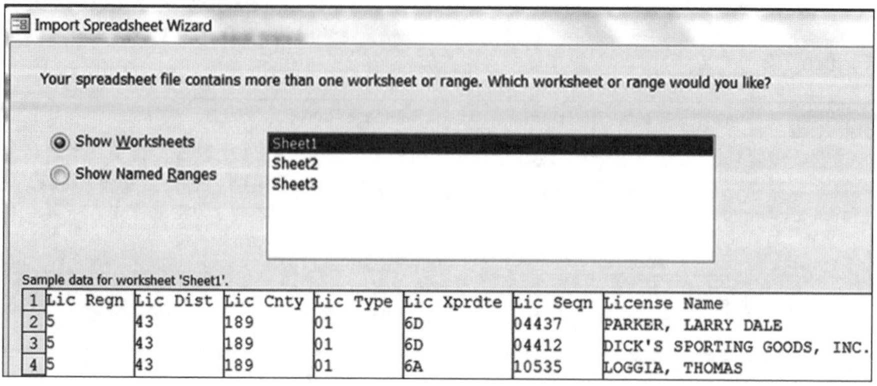

Without the right data, you can't report as accurately and completely on a story. Finding and importing data can be tricky at times, but it's an integral part of CAR. The good news is that the more you do it, the easier it will become.

CAR Wars

It took a strong stomach to successfully pull off our "Restaurant Reservations" series, not to mention oodles of computer-assisted reporting resources and considerable tenacity.

We began with several fundamental questions. We wondered whether area restaurants were generally following or failing the rules; whether the government's system of overseeing restaurants was working; and whether the average consumer had any way to distinguish between the safe and unsafe.

Some government agencies resisted our request for inspection data and only relented after official requests, meetings, and follow-up phone calls and e-mails. Even then, some took weeks or months to provide records. The state Department of Health failed to provide complete data for six months and only after we noticed the computer file that it initially provided was incomplete.

Be careful what you ask for, because you just might get it. That's how we felt after the various agencies' data arrived. There were different formats, missing records, duplicate records, and data from ancient computer systems.

But in total we found area restaurants had violated food-safety rules more than 130,000 times over a five-year period, with

20,000 of those as critical. As for enforcement, we found penalties against violators were rare, even when they were proven to have made people sick.

—Rick Linsk, *The St. Paul Pioneer Press*, Minnesota

Chapter Checklist

- You can locate databases by looking for computers on your beat or asking where charts and tabulated numbers in reports come from.
- Federal and state agencies are putting more and more of their database listings online, yet at the same time are denying access to certain information because of security and privacy concerns.
- Consultants and auditors identify databases in their reports that you might not know about otherwise.
- Always get proper documentation for a database, and always try to get the database for free.
- Know the laws relating to electronic access so that you can use them to your advantage or avoid invoking them.
- Most spreadsheet and database manager software can import most files.

Your Turn to Practice

1. Prepare to request electronic information from the local city or county for names, titles, departments, and salaries for all employees. Make a checklist of what you need.
2. Go to the Reporters Committee for Freedom of the Press Website (www.rcfp.org) and check out the resources available there.
3. Read your state's open records law. Make notes.
4. Check your state attorney general's Website for any opinions relating to your request.
5. Request the record layout of a database of salary information and code sheets.
6. Ask to see a printout of some of the records.
7. Be prepared to write an open records request in case you are asked for one.
8. Import the data into a database manager.
9. Analyze and find out who gets paid the most and what the average and median wage is.

Building Your Own Database

How to Develop Exclusive Sources

> *We wanted to examine how Swedish authorities attacked financial crime in their country. We built our own database of complaints and suspects from three agencies and by looking through several hundred records built the profile of the average suspect and complaint. We determined that the authorities were not pursuing big time crooks, but instead sitting back and dedicating their time to prosecuting small business owners with bookkeeping trouble.*

> —Swedish broadcasters Helena Bengtsson and Jenny Nordberg

By building their own database, Bengtsson and Nordberg joined hundreds of other reporters in the United States and throughout the world over the past two decades in learning to effectively create databases for better journalism. Knowing how to build a database is a skill that helps journalists practicing computer-assisted reporting (CAR) because it means they don't have to rely only on databases created by others.

Journalists outside the United States often have significantly less access to data in their countries and find that they need to get paper records and enter information from those records into a spreadsheet or database manager. But U.S. journalists—especially in small towns—have to create databases much more often than you might suppose.

There are many times when the information you want—especially on the local level—is not in a usable electronic form. Furthermore, despite open records laws, recalcitrant officials may not obey those laws, as discussed in Chapter 7. Those officials may delay their responses to requests, cite privacy and security issues to deny access to public data, or set high prices to limit such access.

Consequently, when you can't obtain data in a timely manner, you might have to take up the challenge of building your own databases. Sometimes, creating your own database is quick and easy. However, data entry and checking the accuracy of data entry can be tedious and time-consuming. To build any database requires some forethought, efficient scheduling, and determination.

But the payoff is well worth it. You will know intimately how accurate the information is. You will start with the database you really need for the story, not a database that will have to be worked with extensively to find what you need. You also can enter the information you want in the most usable format for you. And it provides you with exclusive and frequently powerful stories in which you can report with authority, citing patterns and trends that otherwise would have gone unnoticed. Last, the knowledge of how to build a database makes you a more valuable member of your news organization. Clearly, this is a skill worth having.

Over the past three decades numerous journalists have built their databases on a wide range of international, national, and local issues. Examples include databases on deaths from the terrorist attacks on the World Trade Center, fatalities at race car events, the resale of badly damaged salvage vehicles, questionable pawnshop transactions, employee attendance problems at county agencies and courthouses, sentencing of criminals, the abuse of immigrant workers, lobbyists' gifts to legislators, and the backgrounds of riverboat pilots.

Some journalists build databases to keep track of contacts and sources. Jo Craven McGinty, an expert in CAR and a Pulitzer Prize winner, not only did extensive data analysis on police shootings while at *The Washington Post*, but she also kept a database log of contacts with other metropolitan police departments across the United States. When those department officials claimed to forget she had requested information, she could—by referring to her database—cite the date, time, and person she had talked to the last time she called. In many cases, the police officials became more cooperative when confronted with that information.

While at *The Hartford Courant*, in Connecticut, I built databases on environmental pollution, lobbyists, campaign finance, and early retirement pensions. However, a database I and two other reporters created on murders possibly involving a serial killer resulted in stories with high impact.

Hearing that police were looking at potential links between two or three murders of women in the Hartford area, I decided to look at newspaper clippings of unsolved murders of women in Connecticut during the past five years. There were about forty cases, and we decided to enter demographic information about the victims in a database manager to see if there were any apparent connections. We included the name of each victim, how she was killed, where she was from, and when her body was found. Not all of the information was available. Still we had enough to work with. We started to filter the information by selecting the town the victim was from.

The town in which a body is found dictates which police department investigates. This means that if a killer disposes his victims in different towns, then police may be slower to recognize the link between the crimes than if the killer is disposing of the victims in just one town. The local police and medical examiner's office had been investigating the homicides by the town in which each victim *was found*. By looking at the town the victim *was from*, we discovered a pattern.

To see that pattern, I ran a query to find out how many of the victims were from the city of Hartford. By looking at the detailed information on these individuals, I found that seven of the women had last been seen in the same neighborhood of Hartford, as shown in **Figure 8.1**.

Figure 8.1

	A	B	C	D	E	F
1	Lastname	Firstname	AGE	Street	TownFrom	TownFound
2	MAYO	TAMEIKA			HARTFORD	ROCKY HILL
3	TERRY	CARLA			HARTFORD	WINDSOR
4	RIVERA	SANDRA			HARTFORD	SOUTH WINDSOR
5	DANCY	DIEDRE			HARTFORD	HARTFORD
6	PEREZ	EVELYN			HARTFORD	WETHERSFIELD
7	PEEBLES	PATRICIA			HARTFORD	NEWINGTON
8	PARRENO	MARIA			HARTFORD	HARTFORD

We looked at further details of the crimes, interviewed family members, and gathered more information from a medical examiner's database and from the FBI supplementary homicide database. We also found two other clusters of murders in the state. As a result of our findings, law enforcement officials formed a task force to study possible connections between all the killings, which until then had not been linked.

Within a year, some law enforcement officials were convinced that not one but three serial killers were operating in the state. Officials arrested one suspect and stepped up their investigations. More important, the Hartford killings stopped.

Other reporters have also created databases for their stories. As mentioned in Chapter 2, Mike Berens, then at *The Columbus Dispatch* in Ohio, created his own database and used similar techniques to track an interstate highway serial killer around the same time we were working on the Hartford killings. Reporters at *The Seattle Times* in Washington also created a database on serial killings in their area. In each of these cases, the database provided tips, illustrated possible patterns, and provided a significant stepping-off point for the journalists.

When to Build

 Anthony DeBarros, who helped create a database on victims of the terrorist attacks at the World Trade Center, said that *USA Today* decided to go forward because the reporters knew at a minimum that a verified list of victims' identities would help with follow-up stories and could provide the basis for enterprise work. Indeed, the newspaper broke stories showing with scrupulous detail how the location of a person's office, along with the building design, affected his or her chance of survival. The database also provided leads on survivors, stories on rescue efforts, and many other stories. In addition, it allowed the newspaper to deal with the confusing and possibly erroneous information that government agencies had about the victims.

"Confronted with such a complex web of facts . . . a database is truly the best tool for unearthing trends that make for compelling stories," DeBarros said.

Deciding to build a database should be based on a group of factors. Among them:

- Certainty that the information does not already exist in some kind of electronic form.
- A minimum purpose or a minimum story for which the database can be used, whether it is to keep track of complex information over time or to provide the context for at least one important story.

- Whether the database will be a useful archive and whether reporters can add to it to for future stories.
- How many categories (columns or fields of information) will be required and how many records will have to be entered.
- A realistic estimate regarding the personnel and time needed to create the database.

Once you consider those factors, you can make a well-informed decision about whether to begin.

Spreadsheet or Database Manager

For smaller amounts of information, a spreadsheet is a good tool with which to build a database. A spreadsheet doesn't require first creating a structure in which to enter the data. What you see is what you get. (You can type in the information into a worksheet from smaller data sets, as shown in Chapter 3.)

This means that it is easy to label the columns (or categories) of information, type in the information, and analyze it right away. But if there are many categories of information (more than twenty or thirty) and many records (more than a few hundred) to be entered, it's worth taking the time to consider working in a database manager.

A database manager is designed to deal with more complex information. It also can streamline data entry by allowing you to use a relational database that enables you to enter basic information once rather than many times. As Chapter 6 shows, data entry of political contributions into two tables meant that the candidates' information did not have to be entered more than one time. Placing data in a database manager also means you have the option of linking your database to other databases created by government agencies or businesses.

Whether you choose a spreadsheet or database manager, the good news is that once information is in electronic columns and rows it can be easily imported into the other software. Since how to put data into a spreadsheet is pretty self-evident, we will focus on creating a database in a database manager.

Using the Database Manager

Many reporters initially build a database to keep track of information about political contributors. A political database might include the contributor's name, street, city, state, amount given, to whom it was contributed, and date of contribution.

In a database manager, you need to set up a structure within which to keep the information. This is the same tool known as a *record layout* discussed in Chapter 7. If the information contains words and numbers, you want the type to be "text," or "character" or "alphanumeric" form.

If it contains numbers that you might want to add, subtract, divide, or multiply, the type should be "numeric." If the information is a date, you want to use the date type; this allows you to calculate the number of days between dates, group by dates, and sort by dates. For example, you might want to see on which dates the most traffic accidents occurred. Or you might want to calculate the actual time served in prison by felons.

Unlike a spreadsheet, where you can type without regard to column width, in a database you need to think about how many spaces or characters a field will take (just like a crossword puzzle). Most last names can be contained in twenty-five characters. The codes used for states are always two characters. ZIP codes can be five or nine (ten if including the hyphen) characters long. If you choose numeric, a database manager generally will make sure you have enough space for the number.

Let's look at how you would set up a structure in a database manager. In Microsoft Access, you would open a new database as in **Figure 8.2**, by opening Access, clicking on "New" and on "Blank database."

Figure 8.2

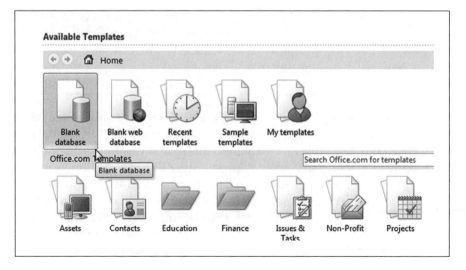

Next, click on "Create" at the top of the screen and then "Table Design," as in **Figure 8.3**.

Figure 8.3

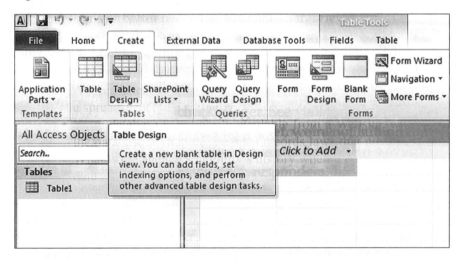

When you select "Table Design," you will get a screen with a grid on it, as shown in **Figure 8.4**. This is where you will build your own record layout (structure of your database).

Figure 8.4

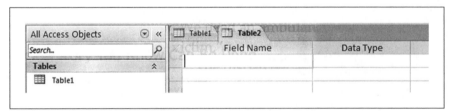

As in Chapter 7, you must be concerned with key areas of the table: the name of the field, the type of data, and the width of the field. Let's create our first table on candidates' information that includes their ID number, name, party, street address, city, ZIP code, election year, and district. (Normally, we would split up the name into at least four fields—last name, first name, middle initial, and suffix—and streets into at least three fields—street number, street name, and street suffix. This ensures that we can sort by any of those fields later. However, for this example, we will take a shortcut—just like many government agencies do.)

Let's name the first field "ID" and choose "Text," as in **Figure 8.5**.

Figure 8.5

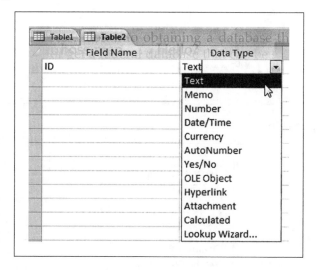

Note that you have many choices of data type. In this chapter, we will use the three major types: text, numeric, and datetime. Also, note that in the lower window, shown in **Figure 8.6**, that "Field Size" (the number of letters or numbers that fit in the field) defaulted to fifty characters. We will change this to "9," since that is the exact amount of numbers that are used in a federal candidate's ID number.

Figure 8.6

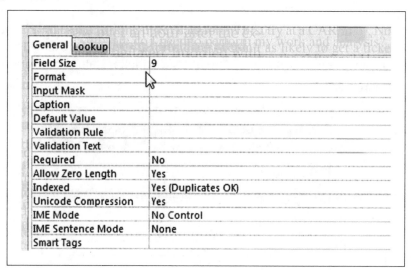

Next, type in "Candidate" for the name, choose "Text," and make the Field Size "50," as in **Figure 8.7a** and **Figure 8.7b**.

Figure 8.7a

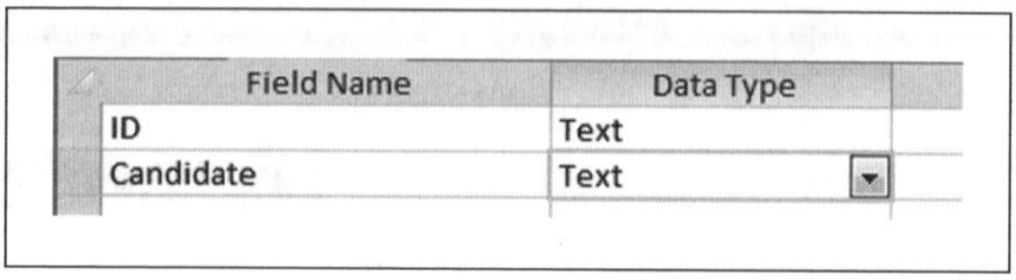

Field Name	Data Type
ID	Text
Candidate	Text ▼

Figure 8.7b

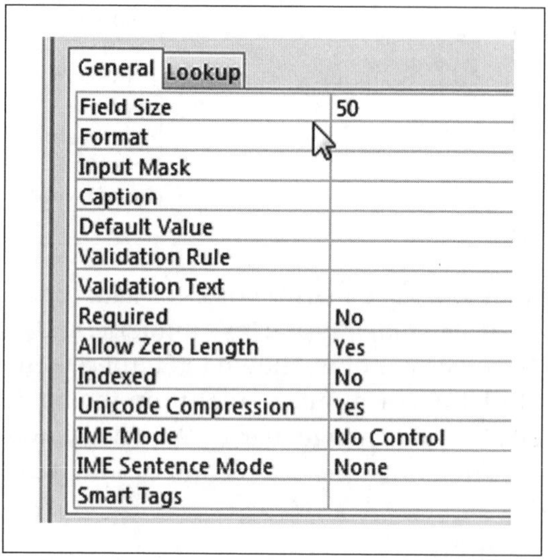

General **Lookup**

Field Size	50
Format	
Input Mask	
Caption	
Default Value	
Validation Rule	
Validation Text	
Required	No
Allow Zero Length	Yes
Indexed	No
Unicode Compression	Yes
IME Mode	No Control
IME Sentence Mode	None
Smart Tags	

Continue putting in field names and deciding on the field size as you go. When you get to "State" as in **Figure 8.8a** and **Figure 8.8b**, for example, change the size to "2" to fit the two-letter state abbreviations.

Figure 8.8a

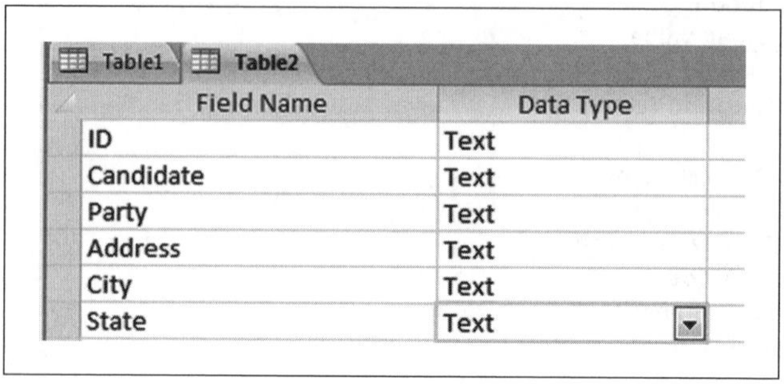

Table1   Table2

Field Name	Data Type
ID	Text
Candidate	Text
Party	Text
Address	Text
City	Text
State	Text ▼

Figure 8.8b

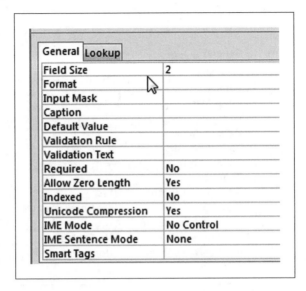

For the next field, "Zipcode," you can specify "5" or "10," since ZIP codes in the United States can be either five digits or nine digits with a hyphen. Keep Zipcode as a text field, because you will never add or subtract the numbers. Also, if you make the Zipcode field numeric and the code starts with a "0," the program may eliminate this digit, and you will have a meaningless four-digit ZIP code (see **Figure 8.9a** and **Figure 8.9b**).

Figure 8.9a

Field Name	Data Type
ID	Text
Candidate	Text
Party	Text
Address	Text
City	Text
State	Text
Zipcode	Text

Figure 8.9b

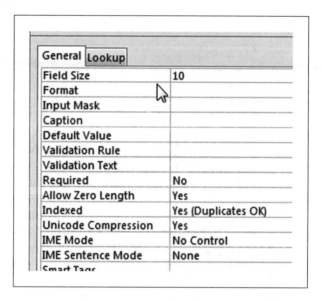

You can now finish the table by typing in "Year" (for the election year) and "District." Year is two spaces, and the field size for District is two spaces. Go to "File" on the menu bar and click on "Save As." Then, type in the name "CANDIDATES" for the new table, as in **Figure 8.10**.

Figure 8.10

Field Name	Data Type
ID	Text
Candidate	Text
Party	Text
Address	Text
City	Text
State	Text
Zipcode	Text
Year	Text
District	Text

Save As

Table Name:

CANDIDATES

OK   Cancel

When you click "OK," the program will ask if you want to create a "primary key." This means that it will automatically give each record a number you might use to link with other tables. In this case, each candidate will already have an ID number, so click on "No" (see **Figure 8.11**).

Figure 8.11

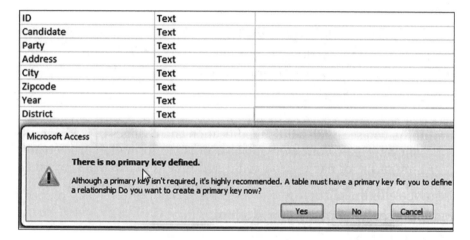

When you click on "No," you can return to the original screen that you started from, and there is your CANDIDATES table (see **Figure 8.12**).

Figure 8.12

All Access Objects	Table1	CANDIDATES
Search...	**Field Name**	**Data Type**
Tables	ID	Text
CANDIDATES	Candidate	Text
Table1	Party	Text
	Address	Text
	City	Text
	State	Text
	Zipcode	Text
	Year	Text
	District	Text

Double-click on "CANDIDATES," and you will go to a screen where you can begin typing in data just as you do in a spreadsheet. You can fill in the fields in each record in any order that you want to, as in **Figure 8.13**, and enter entire records in any order you want because using a database manager makes the data so flexible and easy to sort.

Figure 8.13

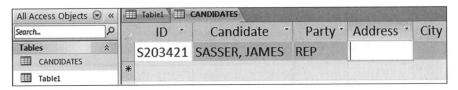

As you see, with a little modification and changes in field names, you can create your own database of any information or keep any kind of list of names. You could add dates of birth, ages, or other demographic information such as ethnicity and gender.

Creating a Relational Database

A single table is sometimes called a *flat file* because it doesn't connect with other tables. In the example of campaign finance, however, we know that we want to add another table and link it to the candidates' names through the candidates' ID numbers.

Once again, we click on "Create" and "Table Design." When we come to the grid, we want to type in the field names: LASTNAME, RESTOFNAME, CITY, STATE, ZIP, OCCUPATION, CONT_DATE (for contribution date), AMOUNT, and CAND_ID. We use the underscores so that the program sees the field name as one word. (Sometimes, database managers, particularly when using Structured Query Language, have problems with spaces.)

The CAND_ID, as in Chapter 6, is the key field linking the CANDIDATES table to the new table, which we will call the GIVERS table. **Figure 8.14** shows what the GIVERS table looks like when completed.

Figure 8.14

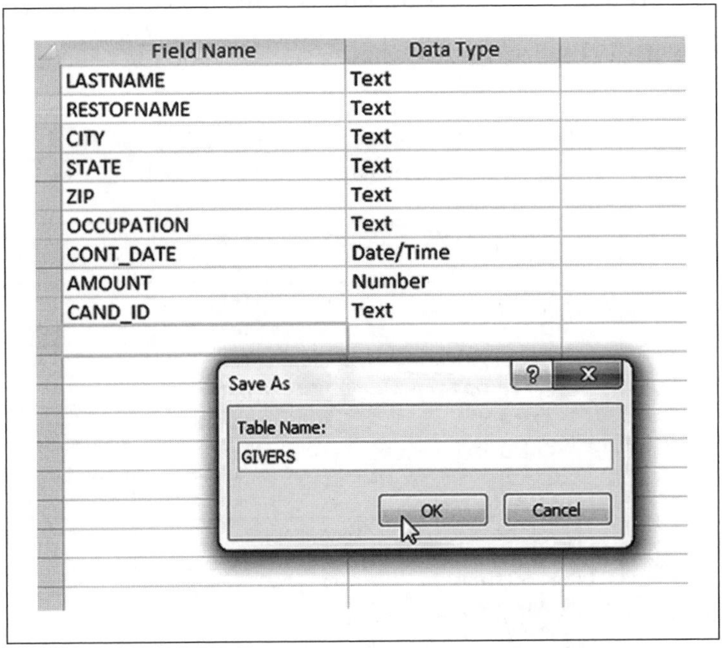

Field Name	Data Type	
LASTNAME	Text	
RESTOFNAME	Text	
CITY	Text	
STATE	Text	
ZIP	Text	
OCCUPATION	Text	
CONT_DATE	Date/Time	
AMOUNT	Number	
CAND_ID	Text	

Save As

Table Name:

GIVERS

OK   Cancel

Note that under Data Type, we put Date/Time next to CONT_ DATE because that field will contain the date the contribution was made. By having the Data Type in the Date format, we can calculate the differences in dates or other analyze a range of dates.

Note, we chose Number for Data Type for the Field "AMOUNT," since we plan to do math—addition and subtraction—with the numbers in that field. We also can limit the amount that can be typed in through the use of the Validation Rule line. This line says data entered outside the limits is not valid.

Most campaign finance laws limit the amount of contributions an individual can make to a single candidate. Let's say, in this example, that you can't give more than $2,000. By typing in <2001 in the Validation Rule line, we can make sure we don't type a number higher than that when doing data entry. (If there is a higher number on a hard-copy report from which you are typing, either you have found an error in how someone recorded the contribution or you have uncovered a very interesting story.) In addition, you can type a message in the Validation Rule line that will show up if you make a mistake. **Figure 8.15** shows these additions to the table.

Figure 8.15

Field Name	Data Type
LASTNAME	Text
RESTOFNAME	Text
CITY	Text
STATE	Text
ZIP	Text
OCCUPATION	Text
CONT_DATE	Date/Time
AMOUNT	Number
CAND_ID	Text

General | Lookup

Field Size	Long Integer
Format	
Decimal Places	Auto
Input Mask	
Caption	
Default Value	
Validation Rule	<2001

Tab1e1 CANDIDATES GIVERS

After closing the window and saving the changes, we can try typing 3000, for $3,000, into the AMOUNT field. When we try to enter the data, we get the message shown in **Figure 8.16**.

Figure 8.16

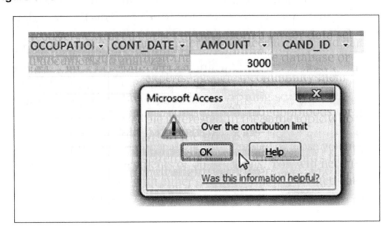

Now that you have created two tables, you can begin the data entry. By keeping the candidates' ID numbers consistent, you have established a relational database. If you create a new query in your database, you can add the two tables to your query screen and link them through their ID numbers, just as we did in Chapter 6 (see **Figure 8.17**).

Figure 8.17

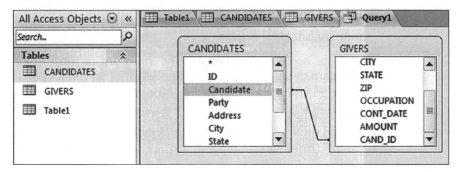

These are the basic steps in creating your own database. With a little practice, you will see constant opportunities to create small or large databases for stories. These databases will lead to tips and much better documented stories or just better record keeping.

CAR Wars

River pilots have one of the most dangerous jobs in Louisiana, but we didn't think the issue was as provocative when we first decided to take a look at the people who guide foreign-flagged vessels along the Mississippi River.

At the time, we wanted to find out if two rumors were true: that Louisiana pilots are some of the highest paid mariners in the country and widespread nepotism makes it virtually impossible for non-relatives to join the ranks.

The main records we wanted were their job applications and the accident reports they filled out. We wound up with six boxes of documents, and we took three weeks to type everything we needed into Excel spreadsheets.

The results were irrefutable: Of the 100 people selected to become river pilots in recent years, 85 were related to other pilots.

We further analyzed our own database with both Excel and Access and found serious problems with overall pilot discipline involving lack of punishment and drug abuse.

—Jeffrey Meitrodt, *The Times-Picayune*, New Orleans

Chapter Checklist

- Database managers allow you to build your own tables of information.
- In building your own tables you can ensure the data is accurate and will serve the needs of your story.
- When building your database, you must plan ahead. You want to ensure that it will have a minimum purpose that will justify the time spent constructing it.
- If you build a good database, it will organize your record keeping, provide tips for stories, and permit you to see and analyze trends and patterns.
- When building a table, always think of possible key fields that will allow you to link the table to other tables.

Your Turn to Practice

1. Using Excel, build a database of your family and friends with their last name, first name, middle initial, street number, street name, street suffix, city, ZIP or mail code, phone number, e-mail, date of birth, sex, and age. Enter at least ten records.
2. Find the average age and median age in your table of family and friends.
3. Using Access, build a table of your family and friends. Enter at least ten records.
4. Find the average age in your table. (Hint: You can find average when you use the Totals line in your queries.)

Fact-Checking the Database

How to Find and Clean Dirty Data

9

When the statewide information on Florida designer-drug deaths arrived, it quickly became obvious that the study was riddled with mistakes. In case after case, the victims appeared too young or too old to be designer-drug users. And records showed that it was unlikely that many of the cases had been scrutinized before. Those cases included terminal cancer patients who shot themselves, nursing home patients who fell, and a four-year-old boy treated for spinal meningitis.

—Hanque Curtis, *The Orlando Sentinel*

Once you start using these computer-assisted reporting (CAR) techniques, it won't be long before you hear and say, "How dirty is the data?" Or to be grammatically correct (most style books treat *data* as a plural noun) "How dirty *are* the data?"

Dirty data usually begins with sloppy typing. Remember that someone who was doing one of the most boring jobs in the world has entered the information in a database. Agencies and businesses generally pay low wages to data-entry clerks, which can create low morale. Often, an agency is too understaffed to do proper data integrity checks. If the agency does do integrity checks, there is still the possibility of erroneous information not being corrected. In addition, the agency should put in *validation rules*, that is, set up an entry system that limits what can be entered into a database. Even in the

173

best-case scenarios, it is surprising how many typos and errors can slip into databases.

Whenever you obtain a new database, always browse through the top 100 records to look for misspellings, omissions, and nonsense. You also should run Group By queries in a database manager that uses pivot tables in spreadsheets to see patterns of bad data entry. For example, if the database contains city names, run a query that asks how many distinct spellings there are. (Often the same town is spelled in several different ways.)

A U.S. Small Business Administration (SBA) database on government guaranteed business loans always seems to have errors in names of cities. If you use a pivot table to count loans in cities in Illinois, you will see a number of spellings for the same city. In **Figure 9.1,** you can see that the city of Arlington Heights has seven different spellings.

Figure 9.1

61	ARLINGTON HEIGHT	1
62	ARLINGTON HEIGHTS	286
63	ARLINGTON HGTS	1
64	ARLINGTON HTS	16
65	ARLINGTON HTS, IL.	1
66	ARLINGTON HTS.	5
67	ARLINGTRON HEIGHTS	1

This level of inaccuracy impairs your ability to perform accurate counts and analysis, unless you clean the data or do manual calculations. Remember that to a computer, a space and a hyphen make the information look different. To a database manager, even "St. Louis" with a period and "St Louis" without a period are different cities.

The lesson is that you must never implicitly trust the data. No database is perfect. No database is complete. Every database is likely to contain a misleading or tricky field. Indeed, George Landau, an early CAR expert, once said that all databases are bad databases. You just have to find out how bad they are, what their flaws are, and determine if they have enough accurate data to be helpful.

For example, the organization EveryBlock, which uses local government data to generate online maps, misplaced crimes in Los Angeles, California, by failing to do accuracy checks. The *Los Angeles Times* did check the data and caused the police department and EveryBlock to make corrections. The *Los Angeles Times* also did an excellent question and answer with EveryBlock founder Adrian Holovaty on the need to check the integrity of data.

Good journalists have always known that they shouldn't trust what anyone tells them until they check the information. (The cliché is that even if your mother tells you she loves you, you should check it out.) That same skepticism must be applied to databases. The world is not a perfect place. People are not perfect. If we are working on a story, we try to determine how much one person knows and then interview another two or three individuals to cross-reference and verify what we were told. We should apply these same methods to databases.

Before you begin the traditional reporting, it is essential to run data checks and decide if you need to clean the data. If so, you also need to decide how much of it to clean. Without doing this first, you will be misled just as though a source gave you the wrong tip.

Another cautionary tale for any journalist working with data involves the unintentional trap in a U.S. government contract database in the years prior to 2001. The database contained items such as which agency awarded a contract, which company received it, the amount, the year, and the place where work on the contract would be carried out.

Lurking in the database was a field of information called "ObligationType." That field (or column as it would be known in Excel) contained one character of information—either "A" or "B." That field followed right after the field for "Dollars," or amount of the contract. (The "A" in the layout stands for the data type, Alphanumeric. The "A" in the data was the character "A.") Part of the actual layout is shown in **Figure 9.2**.

Figure 9.2

Federal Procurement Database			
Data Element	Data	Chars	Position
Dollars (in thous)	N	8	315-322
ObligationType	A	1	323

If you did not pay attention to the "ObligationType" field, you could end up with completely erroneous data. Why? Because all of the dollar amounts posted in the contract database were positive. If the obligation type was identified as "A," the dollar amount remained positive. But if obligation type was "B," the contract was de-obligated, that is, withdrawn, and the dollar amount was supposed to be read as negative. (This meant that you had to multiply the dollar amount by −1 before including it in calculations.)

There was no problem if you knew to ask what "ObligationType" meant or if the agency that distributed the data told you its meaning, but that was not always the case. In fact, several journalists narrowly dodged a major error in the total value of contracts only because they thought to recheck the database, compare it with paper summary reports, and check back with the agency when they saw hundreds of millions of dollars of difference between their totals and those in the government reports.

If they had neglected to multiply dollar amounts by −1 when "ObligationType" was "B," they would have been off by those hundreds of millions of dollars when they did their stories. Lessons learned from that experience were:

- Pay attention to every field and whether it affects another.
- Do an outer integrity check and compare your calculated totals with others' totals.
- Ask questions when the data does not make sense.

Kinds of Pitfalls

Dirty databases and shoddy documentation come in many forms. Among the bugaboos:

- Inaccurate record layouts, code sheets, and record counts.
- Typos or a lack of standardization in the spelling of names and places in the database.
- Incomplete data entry.
- Programming characters such as icons or blanks in the data.
- Data with extra headers copied from a file that was meant to be a printout.
- Inaccurate importing or downloads by the agency or the journalist.

These problems are more common than they should be. However, they can be identified and often corrected.

Two Rules

Before we look at these problems and the solutions, there are two rules in dealing with dirty data.

First, never work on the original database. Create a copy of the database and do your work there. If you make a mistake, you want to be able to recover and start again. You can't do that if you changed the original file. Also, as you work with the data, save each major change to the data as a different file, using a different file name with sequential numbering. This creates an audit trail of your work. For example, working with census data, your first census file might be "states1." The copy would be "states2." The next version would be "states3."

Second, if you need to standardize spellings, never do it in the original field or column. Always create a new field next to it. That way you don't change the original, which can act as a reference point with which you can check your cleaning.

Record Layout

In the previous chapters, we have discussed why you need a record layout if you are going to acquire a database. As we have said, the record layout acts as a road map to the database. It tells you the name of the field of information; whether the field contains letters and numbers, just numbers, or dates; and the width of the column, which indicates how many letters or numbers can fit.

We also discussed the fact that you need the code sheet or codebook that goes with the database. Without the codes, you cannot know, for instance, that "1" means white or that in another field "4" means felony.

You may have to push for months to obtain a database, and once you have it, you will be pleased you won the battle. Unfortunately, you may find that obtaining the database is only the beginning of the struggle to having usable data.

Record Layout Miscues

It is not uncommon for journalists doing CAR to discover not only entry errors in the records but also problems with the record layout and the codebook. Moreover, there is no guarantee that every field has data in it.

For example, FBI annual crime statistics for Chicago have not listed rapes. Due to a disagreement over the definition of rape, the FBI's database has a value of "0" for rapes in Chicago instead of accepting the city's figures.

Moreover, state bail and county databases often lack the critical information about whether a defendant *could* post bond and get out of jail. Sometimes, the agency has removed or redacted the information without saying so.

Let's look at some of the possible problems in record layouts. The sample layout in **Figure 9.3** shows how the information might appear within the columns.

Figure 9.3

Field	Type	Length
First name	Character	15
Last name	Character	20
Agency	Character	20
Salary	Numeric	6

In this example, you would review the information before importing it into your database manager, starting with the first two records, which are shown in **Figure 9.4**.

Figure 9.4

Paul	Jones	Social Services	15541	10/12/2011
Dawn	Brown	Comptroller	21203	05/06/2012

Already, it is apparent that something is wrong. According to **Figure 9.3**, which is the record layout, there should be only four columns of information. But in **Figure 9.4**, there is an extra column of information that looks like a date. What probably happened is that when the database was first put together, the database designer decided not to include the date of hire. Later, the designer thought the date of hire should be added.

When you are ready to import information into your database manager, you may have to set up the structure to hold the information. As you saw in the last chapter, the database structure generally is a mirror of the record layout.

In this example, the database structure you set up (shown in **Figure 9.4**) would look like a record layout. But if you imported the information shown in **Figure 9.4** into that layout, it would fall into the wrong fields. The first few records might look like those shown in **Figure 9.5**. As you can see, the information has shifted and is now falling into the wrong fields.

Figure 9.5

Firstname	Lastname	Agency	Salary
Paula	Jones	Social Services	15541
10/20/91	Dawn	Brown	Comptroller

A real-life instance of the problem of shifting information happened not to a journalist but to the federal court system in Connecticut. In Hartford, the court system made use of a voter list to send out notices for jury duty. To get people's names, the court imported a voter registration list into a database it created. Well, Hartford has a large minority population, whereas towns outside Hartford are largely white. Lawyers soon started to notice that the prospective jurors for federal court were mostly white.

Eventually, an investigation found that data processors for the court had created the wrong record layout for voter registration. Instead of allowing eight spaces for the town's name, Hartford, they allowed only seven spaces. Thus, when the voter registration list was imported into the database, "Hartford" was chopped off at "Hartfor." The truncation would not have been a problem, except that the following field gave the person's life status. Because the field length was too short, the "d" just moved into the next field. In that field, "d" stood for "dead."

Of course, the court didn't want to send jury summonses to dead people, so it had created a program that did not include (filtered out) anyone with a status of "d" on its mailing list. To the court's computer, everyone in Hartford was dead; therefore, no one from Hartford received a jury summons. The result was that there were few people of color on the juries.

Clearly, it is important to check the record layout against the actual data. It is not uncommon to be given an outdated record layout or an incomplete one.

Cryptic Codes

Probably more common than a bad record layout is an incomplete or inaccurate code sheet. In the previous chapter, you learned why you need the code sheet or codebook. The codes must be translated, or you'll be lost in a forest of numbers. But first you need to make sure the codes are accurate.

Let's say you obtain a code sheet that defines ethnicity by numbers: "1" for white, "2" for black, "3" for Hispanic, "4" for Asian American, and "5" for Native American. Once you have imported the information into your database, you perform a standard integrity check. You run a query or use a pivot table that asks for the number of records for each race. The result is shown in **Figure 9.6**.

Figure 9.6

Ethnicity	Totals
1	550
2	430
3	255
4	77
5	88
6	3
7	2
8	1
9	113

What's going on? Why are there so few totals for ethnic groups 6, 7, and 8? And why are there so many for 9? What categories of ethnicity are these? Well, the values for 6, 7, or 8 could be data-entry errors. No one can type hundreds or thousands of numbers without getting at least a few wrong.

After calling the agency and confirming that those values are the result of data-entry errors, you probably will decide to discard those records for purposes of analysis, or simply categorize them as erroneous. But the larger value for the code 9 cannot be ignored. You call the agency again and learn that they have decided to use 9 when ethnicity information wasn't submitted. But they forgot to put that on their code sheet.

In another example, you might be given all the expenditures for every agency in a state. The agencies are listed not by name but by identification numbers, which range from 1001 through 4999. You run a query in which you group the identification numbers and sum the amount column. **Figure 9.7** shows what the first few records might look like.

Figure 9.7

Agency	Total (in thousands)
1022	255,321
4077	121,444
5019	23,655

The result includes an agency identification number, 5019, that does not exist on the code sheet. This kind of anomaly crops up more often than you might expect. For example, states often eliminate and add agencies after the election of a new governor. If agencies are eliminated, their records might still exist in the database, while their code numbers are no longer on the code sheet. If agencies are added, new identification numbers may be added to the database but not to the code sheet. If they are added to a code sheet, they may only be a collection of scribbles on the database administrator's own copy.

Sorry, Wrong Number

As stated above, it's easy to make mistakes in the millions. Therefore, it is essential that you check to see that all the numbers add up, or at least come close. In the previous chapter, you learned (1) to ask how many records you would receive in a database, and (2) to ask for hard-copy reports.

Again, you also need to do an outer integrity check, which means comparing your analysis to a source outside of the database, such as a written summary report by the agency or an auditor. In the example of the federal contracts database, you would group the agencies and sum the dollars. Then, you would compare the sum for each agency with a hard-copy report.

An outer integrity check not only protects against errors but can lead to excellent news stories. Elliot Jaspin, a pioneer in CAR, performed a simple integrity check when he received a database of low-interest mortgages given out by a state agency to low- and moderate-income people in Rhode Island. Working at the *Providence Journal-Bulletin* at the time, Jaspin totaled the amount of mortgages in the database and compared his figure to the totals published in an annual report. The difference was millions of dollars.

As it turns out, Jaspin had not made a mistake. Apparently, the agency had been hiding a slush fund out of which it made loans to the unqualified friends and relatives of politicians. A phone call to the agency from Jaspin about the discrepancy worried those involved, and they began shredding documents. Soon thereafter, the state police raided the agency, and investigations ensued.

Dollar amounts are not the only things that can go awry. One quick outer integrity check can involve counting the number of records in your database and comparing it with the number the agency said it gave you. If the numbers don't match, you have a serious problem, and the situation can be even worse. When it is worse, you need to think of all the integrity checks you can perform.

I once asked for attendance records for 10,000 state employees. The records showed how the employees spent every working hour—whether it was regular time, overtime, sick time, vacation, or personal days. The agency that gave me the records said it had forgotten to do a record count; but because it gave me 1.8 million attendance records, which is what I had counted, I thought I had them all.

After a while, however, it occurred to me that I probably should have records for at least 250 days for each employee. Even if an employee left partway through the year, another employee would be earning overtime. A quick calculation of 10,000 employees times

250 days results in 2.5 million records. It took two days of debate, but the agency finally took a look at its own work, found a serious programming error, and acknowledged that it had shorted me by 700,000 records. It sent me the 700,000.

Where Is the Standard?

One of the most onerous database problems is the lack of standardization. Names can be spelled several different ways, and different words may be used for the same category, such as "attorney" or "lawyer" in the Federal Election Commission (FEC) contributor database. It can be time-consuming to fix these problems, but sometimes it's the only way to go if you want to get accurate counts and summaries.

Let's go back to the SBA database and fix the Arlington Heights problem. One way to do it is in a database with the basic concept of fixing dirty data. You simply use the Find and Replace function in Excel, as shown in **Figure 9.8.**

Figure 9.8

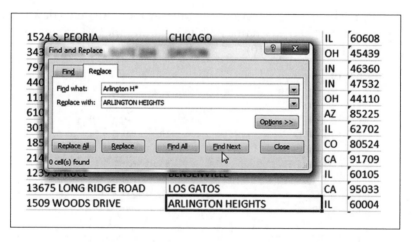

Not only is it tedious (and any data cleaning can be drudgery), but even using a wild card "*" still takes you to address columns where there is an Arlington Road. Furthermore, you are not making corrections in a new column; you would have to work in a new worksheet and then compare back to the original.

A faster and more reliable way is to use the Update command in a database manager like Access. First, you need to create a new field, called "NewCity," in the Table Design view (see **Figure 9.9**).

Figure 9.9

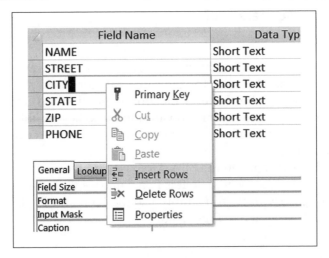

By clicking on "Insert Rows," you now have created a new field to put standardized city names while retaining the old names to check against (see **Figure 9.10**).

Figure 9.10

Field Name	Data Type
NAME	Short Text
STREET	Short Text
NEWCITY	Short Text
CITY	Short Text
STATE	Short Text
ZIP	Short Text

General	Lookup
Field Size	255
Format	

Once you have a new field, you can use an "update" statement in a query to define all possible spellings of the name and tell the database manager to change the names to one spelling and to put the changes in "NEWCITY." To use "Update," go through the process of getting to the query window in Access, calling up the SBAILLINOIS table through Show Table; go to the menu bar and click on "Query"; and then click on "Update," as shown in **Figure 9.11**.

Figure 9.11

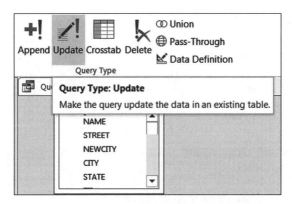

As a result, you get a form in the lower window that you fill out with what you want to change. You update the new field, NEWCITY, with the standard and correct spelling of Arlington Heights and then in the old field CITY you use the criteria line to put in "Like arlingt*" to catch the right spelling and the wrong spellings, as shown in **Figure 9.12**.

Figure 9.12

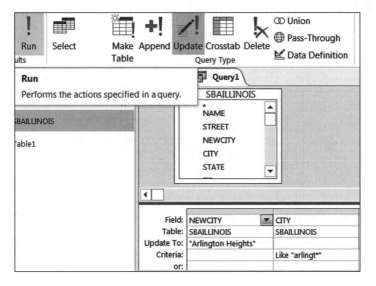

When you run the query as in **Figure 9.13,** you will be asked if you want to insert the changes in the necessary rows. Click "Yes," as shown in **Figure 9.13**.

Figure 9.13

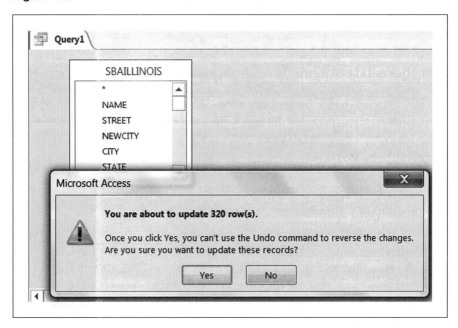

In Structured Query Language, you could write out the query, as in **Figure 9.14**.

Figure 9.14

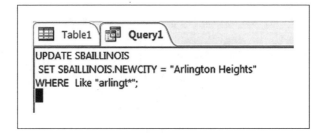

In either case, your data would look like what is shown in **Figure 9.15** with the misspellings of Arlington Heights corrected. You still need to check carefully that you did not mistakenly change a city name.

Figure 9.15

Arlington Heights	ARLINGTON HEIGHTS
Arlington Heights	ARLINGTON HEIGHTS
Arlington Heights	ARLINGTON HEIGHTS
Arlington Heights	ARLINGTON HTS
Arlington Heights	ARLINGTON HEIGHTS
Arlington Heights	ARLINGTON HEIGHTS
Arlington Heights	ARLINGTON HEIGHTS
Arlington Heights	ARLINGTON HEIGHTS
Arlington Heights	ARLINGTON HEIGHTS
Arlington Heights	ARLINGTON HEIGHTS
Arlington Heights	ARLINGTON HGTS
Arlington Heights	ARLINGTON HEIGHTS
Arlington Heights	ARLINGTON HTS

Now, if you wanted to count all the loans in Arlington Heights, you could write a query that used NEWCITY and counted the number of loans, and you would get the correct number this time.

This is only the beginning of data cleaning. But the practice of creating a new field and then putting a standardized spelling in that field is a common practice and frequently necessary.

Header-Aches

You finally persuade an agency to give you information in an electronic form rather than on a printout. You get the record layout and a DVD, or they post it online for you, using an FTP site or a service such as Dropbox. You get the data, open it up in your computer, and browse through the information, and what do you see? A horror show of headers.

Headers are the identifying bits of information that go across the top of a printout page. They may tell you the date, page number, and other information that has no place in your database of columns and rows. An example is given in **Figure 9.16**.

Figure 9.16

Date 0/2/2013 Administrative Services Page 3			
Name	Town	Zip	Salary
Sun, Gerald	Lincoln	06320	35,004
Moon, Mary	Jefferson	93914	42,523

In response, the agency—through incompetence, laziness, or nastiness—apparently gave you the image of each printed-out page instead of the raw data. Fortunately, you can correct the problem with a Word or database manager or a quick program. (We won't go through every step in this handbook, but we'll go over the basic idea of what you can do.)

If you can import the information into a database, you will likely end up with nonsense records at the beginning of each row that starts with "date." For example, the information might look like what you see in **Figure 9.17**.

Figure 9.17

NAME	TOWN	ZIP	SALARY
Date 0/2/2013 Administrative Services Page 3			
Name	Town	Zip	Salary
Sun, Gerald	Lincoln	06320	35,004
Moon, Mary	Jefferson	93914	42,523

But with a "where" statement—such as "delete all records where name like 'Date*'"—you can locate the offending records and eliminate them. In Access, you would go to the query window as you did in updating a table and this time choose "Delete Query." Then you would follow the same process as updating and have a query that looks like **Figure 9.18**.

Figure 9.18

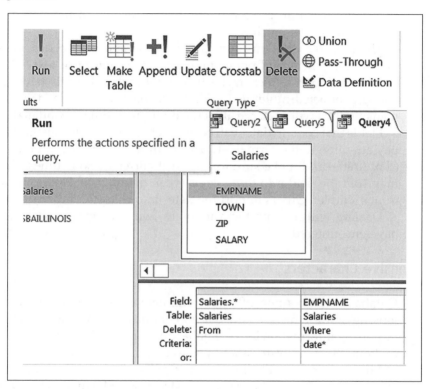

Numbers versus Text

Importing databases incorrectly can lead to cutting off the 0s at the beginning of numbers and create major problems. For example, if a spreadsheet or database manager imports ZIP codes or another identification number into a numeric field that starts with 0, this may lead to significant damage. If the database manager sees a ZIP code that begins with a 0, it will eliminate the ZIP code, because the 0 it looks like a blank to the database manager.

Thus, for journalists who work in ZIP codes that begin with 0 (such as 01776), all ZIP codes will be entered as four characters (1776) instead of five if the format of the cell or field is numeric. Those ZIP codes will be useless not only for mailing addresses but also for matching one database to another.

The same problem can happen with other identification codes. An employee with the identification number 042325 will have it rendered as 42325 if it is put into a numeric field. This is incorrect and also prevents accurate matches.

The way to escape this peril is to always import ZIP codes, identification numbers, and phone numbers into character or text fields. Generally, import as a character field any number that will never be added, subtracted, multiplied, or divided. The spreadsheet or database manager then will preserve all of the digits, including the initial 0.

Fields that contain dates can be another problem. Journalists must pay attention to the format—U.S. (month first) or European format (day first)—and make sure to import it correctly. Sometimes, they may split the field into three fields (year, month, and day) to make things simpler. Others import the dates into character fields.

Dealing with this problem involves two strategies you already have encountered.

Offensive Characters

Databases can contain offensive characters. They may be weird-looking smiling faces or misplaced commas or semicolons. Before importing information into a database, you probably want to get rid of them. Most programs allow you to do this fairly easily.

Microsoft Word will allow you to use its advanced Find function to basically write *search and replace* instructions. The function may be under the "Edit" button in earlier versions of Word or at the far right of the "Home" menu. But wherever it is, you can use it to find and replace characters and punctuation. Say you want to eliminate commas in the data. You would type a comma in the "Find" part of the box and leave "Replace" blank. You then click on "Replace All."

There is a fancier way to do this with database programs, using tools called *string functions* or programming code. String functions are a powerful but sometimes confusing way to clean data. A string is a series of letters or numbers or other symbols, such as commas in a field. A string function is a command that allows you to alter such data in a field.

For example, a string function can enable you to split a field containing a comma or space into two fields. This can be handy when you are trying to match names in one table with names in another. For instance, one table may put the first name in a separate field and the last name in another field. But another table may put the last and first name in the same field, such as "Smith, John." To make the names in the second table useful for a match, you can use the comma as a marker to split the name into a first name and a last name.

This guide does not cover string functions, but the National Institute for Computer-Assisted Reporting has many handouts on functions and programming code, as well as other cleaning programs such as OpenRefine. What's important is that you know this kind of data cleaning is possible.

Parsing

Once again, no database is perfect or complete, but most can be made usable. Parsing has long been a popular way of doing data cleaning in spreadsheets. *Parsing* means drawing column lines between different kinds of data to create separate columns out of what was meant to be one column.

The import wizard you saw in Chapter 2 will look at a text file when you open it and suggest column lines. If the text file is in a tabular format (i.e., it looks like columns), the spreadsheet can rapidly arrange the data. This is especially handy for small files downloaded from online sources. You can draw lines between the text columns by clicking. You can delete them by putting the cursor on the line and double-clicking.

CAR Wars

The Washington Post *series "Deadly Force," which won a Pulitzer Prize, resulted from a close examination of the FBI's Supplementary Homicide Report (SHR). The examination revealed that the SHR data for the country that year did not have a single "81"—the code for a justifiable homicide by a police officer. Neither did any of the other years I checked.*

This suggested that whole records were missing from the dataset. The FBI's own documentation provided another corroborating clue. By comparing the number of records cited on the documentation and the number of records in the database, it was clear that there were 287 fewer records than there were supposed to be.

After conversations with the FBI, I found that they did collect the data but did not make it part of their "standard release." After two requests, the FBI delivered another computer tape that contained hundreds of "81s." The raw numbers were remarkable. Only officers in a handful of cities—all much larger than Washington, D.C.—had shot and killed more people. Ultimately, these records served as a starting point for the series.

—Jo Craven McGinty, *The Washington Post*

Chapter Checklist

- Know how many records are supposed to be in the database.
- Compare total amounts in your database to hard-copy reports.
- Check the data for missing words.
- Make sure that fields containing identification codes and ZIP codes include all of the digits; you can do this by formatting the fields as characters or text.
- Match the record layout carefully to the actual data; check for omissions or deletions.
- Use word processors or string functions in database managers to correct errors.
- When the number of records is small, use spreadsheet parsing to establish connections between records.

Your Turn to Practice

1. Get part of the FEC contributor database or use the database CAMPAIGN that is available at this book's Website.
2. Open your table or the table GIVERS, and copy it as new table called GIVERS2. Using the Design View, create a new field called "Occupation2."
3. Copy all of the occupations in the occupation field into the Occupation2 field.
4. Using the update command, change all "attorneys" entries in Occupation2 to "lawyers." Then change all "physicians" entries to "doctors."
5. Using Occupation2, group the data by occupations and total the amounts of contributions.

Doing the Computer-Assisted Reporting Story

How to Report and Write with Data

> *Computer-assisted reporting is no different than other journalism in an important way: Often the best stories start with a reporter's gut instinct.*

> —David Knox,
> *The Akron Beacon-Journal,* Ohio

You have the computer, the software, and the understanding that the judicious and skillful use of computer-assisted reporting (CAR) techniques can create good news stories. But now what?

If you're not careful, you can suffer a severe case of reporter's block, trying to figure out what stories to write and how to do them. Worse, a large database can swallow you up with its complexities, distracting you from finishing any story. Instead, stop and consider what you have learned in this book.

CAR is not meant to be a separate endeavor, but rather it should be an integral part of the newsgathering process. This ever-increasing part of journalism offers techniques to use and improve and enhance your current reporting, not necessarily take center stage.

Above all, CAR should apply to topics that you are interested in writing about. When you consider using a database or databases for a story, you should contemplate these questions as you learned them in the previous chapters:

- Are there databases relevant to the story that would help with depth, context, or ideas?
- Have you checked online news stories or the Investigative Reporters and Editors (IRE) Resource Center to see if anyone used a database for this kind of story?
- Are the databases available on the Web? Can they be downloaded in usable formats? Is the database composed of more than one file?
- Which software would be appropriate for analyzing the database? A spreadsheet or a database manager? Is the database too large for a spreadsheet?
- If the database is not easily available from a Website, who keeps the database? What are the open records laws that govern its use? What is the agency's or entity's history when it comes to releasing data?
- How could the database be used graphically? Bar charts? Interactive maps? Other visualizations?
- Who are the people you will need to profile and interview for this story so that it is not a "dry data" story?
- How do you ensure that the story will be fair and not distort or misrepresent the statistics and data that you use?

Perhaps, most important is the challenge that goes with all stories. What is the larger question you are seeking to answer with this news story? Will the data help answer that question? You can deal with all of these factors with a few key strategies.

Pick a Story You Know Can Be Done

Review stories that have been done at other news organizations and see if you can apply their approaches and acquire similar databases to illuminate issues in your area. The Resource Center at IRE has thousands of CAR stories indexed at its Website (www.ire.org/resourcecenter).

Many of those stories have been entered into the IRE awards contest and have contest forms that reporters filled out to explain how they did the story, what databases and documents they used, and what challenges they faced. Those contest entries have been scanned by IRE, and you can download and review them.

Pick a Database You Can Get

Quite often, journalists spend most of their time acquiring, cleaning, or building a database when doing a CAR story. To avoid that time-consuming process, look into obtaining a database that has been released before or get a federal database that can be sliced down to the local level.

The National Institute for Computer-Assisted Reporting (NICAR; www.ire.org/nicar/) has more than forty major U.S. databases from which the institute can extract the data for your region. Some databases are useful for any country, but you also can search for data for Websites maintained by your own country or you can download data for your country or region from international Websites such the World Health Organization, the World Bank, or the United Nations.

If you are going to build a database, follow the guidelines in Chapter 8 to avoid getting bogged down in data entry. When you first start out with CAR, it is advisable to keep your first self-built database small and manageable.

Some First-Time Examples

If you want to look at the first stories some reporters did after they learned these techniques, you can check the "first ventures" reported in *Uplink* (www.ire.org/blog/uplink), the authoritative newsletter on CAR:

- Jason Callicoat of *The South Bend Tribune* in Indiana took weather data and parking ticket data for his first try at a CAR story. Not only did he discover that residents weren't as likely to get a ticket on a bad weather day, but he also found that armed forces recruiters owed the city thousands of dollars.
- Edward L. Carter at *The Deseret News* in Utah produced a story illustrating the lack of women in top management positions in local government after getting public data on municipal employees, their salaries, and other employment information.
- Mark Houser of *The Pittsburgh Tribune-Review* in Pennsylvania used Excel worksheets on lottery sales to help report on high sales to working-class families and other social consequences of the state's lottery system.

- Missouri School of Journalism student Mark Greenblatt won an IRE award for using a federal database on the conditions of bridges in Missouri to help him identify deficient and unsafe bridges.
- Other reporters have entered data on jury pools or voter registration, turning around stories in just a few days.

Start Small

It sometimes is a matter of pride for some journalists to use a database composed of hundreds of thousands or millions of records. But for many journalists, some of the most effective stories have come from only a few hundred or thousand records.

Furthermore, starting with a small database allows you to get to know the information. Look for databases that involve only a few columns of names or numbers. If you really have to or want to, you can manually check or spot-check the database; doing so will improve your confidence in the information and in your skills.

In the 1980s and early 1990s, most databases came from mainframe computer tapes. They had to be downloaded and broken up into smaller parts to be used on personal computers. Now, our computers at home can handle enormous databases that can be downloaded, or you can just put your criteria—city and state, for example—in a form online to download only the information you need.

Some large databases, such as census files, are already broken into small databases in Excel. Journalists now routinely use small census files for stories on housing, income, transportation, or ethnic diversity in cities.

Building Your Own

As shown in Chapter 8, it's not that difficult to build your own database. If you do, you immediately take three steps toward a successful story:

1. You automatically are familiar with the information because you obtained and organized the data.
2. Because data entry is so tedious, you will limit the amount of information and keep it relevant.
3. If *you* build a database, then no one else has it, and you may uncover

an exclusive story. Remember that a database doesn't have to have thousands or even hundreds of records. Two of the most useful databases I built had fewer than 150 records each.

Journalists Karl Idsvoog and Corky Johnson set a standard in the early 1990s when they showed the effectiveness of building a database. Their databases resulted in sharp investigative stories, including pieces on the sale of salvaged cars, absenteeism at a county office, and wasteful practices at a local housing agency.

At *The Hartford Courant* in Connecticut, environmental writer Daniel Jones, researcher Leah Segal, and I built an abbreviated database on emissions of toxic chemicals by manufacturers. (This was after we learned that we would have to wait nine months for government officials to release their database.) By doing so, we learned a great deal about how companies filled out the hard-copy reports, and we learned that the state had not mentioned 20 percent of the emissions in its reports because of administrative decisions. For months, no one else had comparable information, and we used the database for several exclusive stories.

Match the Database to Your Knowledge

Although electronic databases permit you to learn and explore new subjects, it's better to get a database on something you know about when you are starting. Building your own database is one way to be sure of the information and how to use it; getting a database on a topic you know about and cover is another way.

A database is a mirror of reality, but a mirror always has flaws. You need to know how flawed the mirror is and how distorted the image. That's why it's good to get a database about your own beat or specialty, and there are numerous databases available online and offline on just about every beat. The database can highlight problems or provide tips about the subject, but you know the context.

If you find flaws in the database, you have to decide whether it is worth cleaning up those flaws and how long that will take. Some databases simply can't be used without some cleanup, and you need to make an assessment of the time and effort that will take before embarking on such a task. If it is a matter of standardizing a location name, then it will be easy to do. If it's matter of parsing one column into three columns it may take more time. But, again, it can be done pretty quickly.

If you aren't reporting on a familiar subject, then team up with a reporter who does know it. When I worked on a judicial story, I worked with the court reporter. On other subjects, I worked with the environmental reporter, the medical reporter, the city hall reporters, or the political reporters. They pointed out problems in the databases and could also discern patterns and clues in the data.

The Minimum Story

When you are starting out, never get a database without thinking about the minimum story. By *minimum story*, I mean the surest, most basic story available. This approach, introduced by legendary investigative editor Robert W. Greene, has been used and taught by veteran journalists for all kinds of reporting.

If you get a database of governmental salaries, you can be pretty sure that you will have a story about the average, the median, and who gets the highest and lowest salaries. If you get a database of housing prices over a span of years, you can be confident that you will have a story about changes and trends. If you get a database on crime, you will undoubtedly be able to report on increases and decreases. If you get a database on political contributions, you will have a story based on who gave the least and most, and where the contributors were from.

These are minimum stories. They don't always become the lead story of the day, but they are solid and enable you to engage in meaningful journalism. They also provide you with a foundation of databases that bolster later stories or can be combined with new databases for even better stories. In addition, they show potential sources that you are interested in the topic.

Keep Up with Other Reporters' Work

Too many journalists get caught up in the argument that a story has been done before. Frankly, most stories have been done before. That's not the point. The real questions are whether your story is a good one, whether the previous stories have been done thoroughly and correctly, and whether your material is of current interest in the geographic area in which you work.

The same applies to using databases. After all, a reporter in one community can do a reasonably good overview of who sells guns in that community. Possibly, there is no shattering news, just an interesting look at the issue. But you may get the same database for your own community and discover that many gun dealers are police officers, and that some of them sell guns to convicted felons. It's the quality of the database and what you do with it that counts.

Therefore, it is important to try to keep up with what other journalists are doing. When you read or hear about a journalist who has used a database or online resources that you may be interested in, review the stories to determine how the sources might be applicable in your own situation. You also can call or e-mail the journalist for tips on the database.

NICAR and IRE offer many resources revealing how journalists have researched CAR stories and what databases and software were used. NICAR's listserv, nicar-l; its Website, *The IRE Journal*; and the newsletter *Uplink* also give how-to information on CAR. Nonprofit investigative reporting centers, such as ProPublica (www.propublica. org), also will explain how they used data for a story.

Integrate Databases into Your Daily Work

Although some journalists use databases only for long projects, you should try to integrate their use into stories on the beat and on the deadline. Indeed, Pat Stith, an inspiring investigative reporter at *The News & Observer* in Raleigh, North Carolina, and a pioneer in CAR, gave a good tip when he said, "We are going to use databases to create or improve everyday front page stories."

The "improve" part of that statement is especially useful for a journalist beginning to explore CAR. Quietly improve your stories by adding online searches, small spreadsheet calculations, and summary data from database managers. By doing so, you will bring depth and context to your daily and beat reporting that will make every story more important and more informative.

Find a Partner

If at all possible, find a partner to learn with. With any new way of thinking and looking at information, it helps to have someone to talk to and discuss solutions to problems. The "buddy system" keeps you focused and also helps prevent errors. Having a friendly colleague look over your shoulder when you are doing your first queries or calculations will save you a great deal of time and trouble. You will also learn faster by helping someone else.

Become Familiar with the Field of Data Processing

Because you are learning a new subject, take the time to read articles and books about computer hardware, software, databases, and programming language. They can help you learn the lingo and find tools that might help you do a better job.

You should also get to know people who work in programming but who are not journalists. They often have a quick answer for a problem that has baffled you and other journalists. In addition to NICAR, an excellent group to join is Hacks and Hackers. (The name is slang for journalists and programmers.) They hold "meetups" that allow for faster exchange of information. Forums on software, social research methods, and public databases also are full of helpful how-to tips and story ideas.

Look for Tips

Keep a narrow focus when you start doing these kinds of stories, but don't overlook potentially good stories or tips in databases. When you have finished your minimum story, set aside a half hour to go back and peruse a database. (Make that a firm half hour by using a timer, or you could pass half a day without realizing it.)

Look for tips by searching for particular words, looking for outliers, creating summary data using Group By, calculating percentages, or just scanning the databases for trends and patterns. Often, a good story can emerge from such a scan of a database.

Writing the Story

Too often, when starting to write the story, reporters let themselves become overwhelmed by the statistics and numbers. You can't write your notebook, as has often been said.

Throughout the reporting process, especially when dealing with data, numbers, and statistics, you will need to think about summarizing. As Sarah Cohen of *The New York Times* has urged, consider these questions: Which is the one most important number that tells the story? Is it a raw number like 5,000? Is it a rate, ratio, or percentage increase?

If possible, the key number should be the only number in the first few paragraphs of a story. Most likely, you will have other numbers, but many of them should be visualized in a chart, graph, or map. Otherwise, the reader or viewer will be overwhelmed. If you think it will provide a service, you also can list all of the numbers on a Website in a separate file.

Once you have the central number, what is the best human example you have? If you lead a story with an anecdote about one case, it should represent the pattern or outliers you found in the data.

Sometimes, in complex stories, you need to explain how you researched the story and what data you used. Separate from the main story, you can provide details on methodology and data, giving your story more credibility. You also can make the entire database available online so that others can review your work, look for other stories, or comment on your work.

In addition, you need to get out and see what you are writing about. If it is toxic dumps, then go look at them. If it is schools, then visit them. If it is small businesses, go there and do interviews. If you do the lab (CAR) work, it is key that you also do the necessary fieldwork and the legwork. And remember that good stories are about people and for people.

Good Reporting and Ethics

Throughout your newsgathering and data work, remember to be accurate and fair. There are plenty of politicians, researchers, and advocates who want much too badly to use and publicize numbers that will back up their positions. As an independent journalist, it is your job not only to expose their manipulation of numbers, but also to prevent yourself from seeing what you hope to see.

Quite often, the story turns out to be even a better one if the database doesn't support your initial hypothesis. Either way, the only good story is one that summarizes accurately what you have found.

As you put together your story, you need to be willing to share the highlights of your findings during your interviews and to listen to and consider contrasting opinions. In addition, keep an eye out for "lurking variables"—that is, additional factors that could potentially skew the meaning of data. It is much better to find out that you are wrong before you publish a story than after the public sees it.

Throughout our story on racial disparity in how bail amounts were set, court reporter Jack Ewing and I constantly tried to play devil's advocate with the data and to come up with arguments against our initial findings. Push your editor or colleagues to help you look at your work critically.

Finally, when the story is complete, go back and recheck your facts line by line. Whenever possible, tie facts back to your data and documents and footnote them as appropriate. And always provide full source information for online or published sources.

Stay Curious, Get Excited

Stay curious and excited about your stories. The lasting attraction of CAR is that you can do stories you never could have done before in ways you never thought of. Moreover, you can be creative and responsible at the same time and provide the public with the best and most accurate view of an issue.

Reporting with CAR

Here is a summary of the steps in doing CAR stories:

I. Begin the story with a hypothesis or question.
   A. Explore a tip from a person or other source.
   B. Group and sort data you already have to show possible trends, patterns, or unusual events.
   C. Observe an event or condition in your community.
II. Draw up a list of persons to interview, places to visit, and databases and documents to analyze.
   A. People can include experts, agencies, community members, and the custodians and users of relevant data.
   B. Places include agencies, businesses, neighborhoods, or sites to which the data refers.
   C. Databases are those that already are created or those you may have to build from documents or observations. You will need the right software to work with either existing or newly created databases.

III. Prioritize your list and compose a schedule for completing the list.
   A. Make all open records requests as early as possible.
   B. Plan to interview certain people—usually administrators—at the beginning of your work if you can, after your first run though the data. (You may need to interview the same people after your site visits, further data analysis, and other interviews—see below.)
   C. Do the data analysis. Look for flaws in the data and your methods.
   D. You may need to do your site visits before the data analysis and after the data analysis. Data analysis will help you focus.
   E. Also take into account the possibility that your list may grow, and you may need to redo your schedule.
IV. Write the story.
   A. Summarize your data work and decide what the key numbers are and what should be visualized in charts or maps.
   B. Summarize your interviews and site visits. Decide who and what are most representative of your reporting and data analysis results.
   C. Check your data findings against outside reports based on the data, and run your findings past experts or persons familiar with the data.
   D. Outline the story and decide on the appropriate tone.
   E. Be prepared to re-interview some people and to redo your data analysis as part of the verification process.
   F. Write the story.
   G. Do a line-by-line check of all of the facts in your story.
   H. Be prepared to defend your methodology.
   I. Plan possible follow-up stories before you publish or air.

CAR Wars

After taking a NICAR boot camp, it wasn't long before I was finding ways to use my newfound skill.

In fact, CAR has become an everyday method for me. When I'm looking for information among the first things I ask is "How are the records kept?" or "How far back do those records date?" The whole process is always an adventure.

For one story, an initial tip on missing school equipment came from a source in the fixed assets department. We then requested from the school an inventory of missing equipment.

They declined to give it to us electronically and instead supplied the list on paper. The list totaled $2.5 million of equipment lost *over a five-year period. I entered all the information on an Excel spreadsheet, added up the totals, calculated percentage increase/loss over time, sorted the data to see which schools were losing the most, and looked at the items that were lost the most frequently. The list included VCRs, computers, televisions, and band equipment. Two of the most unusual items were a John Deere tractor and a walk-in freezer. Our story created quite a stir and a subsequent audit by the school district revealed that the problem was even worse than we reported: $4.2 million in equipment was missing!*

—Joe Ellis, KMOL-TV

Chapter Checklist

- Focus on databases relating to subjects you know.
- Identify existing and available databases that are useful for your story.
- Build your own database as needed. If new to CAR, start small.
- Look at how other CAR stories were done. (Hint: IRE, NICAR, and other sources share information on CAR stories and how they were done.)
- Use the buddy system. A colleague's viewpoint can make all the difference.
- Use databases as tipsters—that is, like people who tip you off to good stories or wrongdoing.
- Integrate CAR into your daily journalism.

Your Turn to Practice

1. Research the IRE Resource Center (www.ire.org/resourcecenter) for CAR stories that have been done.
2. Read journalists' articles, contest entries, or tip sheets kept at IRE to learn about how other journalists used data for their stories.
3. Download three Excel worksheets from the U.S. Census Bureau that have information on topics you are interested in.
4. Get a local slice of data—make sure it is in one table—from the IRE and NICAR data library on infrastructure, transportation accidents, or other issues of interest in your region, and analyze that data.

Appendix A

A Short Introduction to Mapping Data

In this appendix, we take a look at the basic uses of mapping software—known as geographic information systems (GIS)—and some of the techniques you can employ to visualize your data. Mapping data is basically taking columns and rows of information and overlaying that information on geographical maps. By doing this well, you enable yourself, your readers, and other viewers to clearly visualize what the data means.

For example, using mapping software, you can place dots that represent the location of auto accidents on a map of streets. Suddenly, a list of accidents turns into clusters of dots at certain intersections, and you see where the dangerous intersections are.

Mapping data as part of journalism has quickly evolved from the occasional to the routine, and you can find plenty of good examples. It has greatly helped that it has become easier to upload or import columns and rows into GIS software online or on your computer. In addition, more Websites, especially government Websites, allow you to map data online by providing the data and the software on their sites.

Journalists have many different kinds of data mapping software available to them. These include the popular Google Fusion Tables or Google Maps, Tableau, and long-standing Esri products such as ArcGIS and its Microsoft add-on Esri Maps.

As the software has become less expensive and easier to use, reporters throughout the country have used mapping to reveal patterns of criminal drunken driving, bank and insurance discrimination, landslides, migration, environmental hazards, lottery sales, school test scores, blighted buildings, health problems, white flight, and unsafe bridges and dams.

Finding Patterns

Journalists began making revealing displays of data more frequently in the 1990s. When Hurricane Andrew hit Florida in 1992, the damage was enormous and costly. In its aftermath, *Miami Herald* computer-assisted reporter Steve Doig—now a professor at Arizona State University—created a map that overlaid wind speed reports on the locations of 60,000 building inspection damage reports. The visual result was stunning.

A reporter would expect to find that the areas that experienced high wind speeds would have a large amount of building damage and that the areas with lower wind speeds would have less damage. But Doig's map showed that some areas with lower wind speeds had high damage. The map tipped off Doig and other *Miami Herald* reporters about where to start their investigation into poor building and inspection practices, particularly after 1980. That work led to an exposé of incompetence and corruption that won the *Miami Herald* a Pulitzer Prize.

In mapping, data on a topic such as wind speeds is imported into the software. As in a database manager, key fields in the table on wind speeds, such as longitude and latitude, are matched to longitude and latitude in a template table.

"Mapping is just such a quick and useful way of taking what could be an otherwise unintelligible pile of information and finding the patterns in it," Doig said. Doig's and other reporters' ventures inspired thousands of stories throughout the world that have tapped into the power of mapping.

More recently, in 2011, *The Guardian* newsroom in the United Kingdom brought attention to GIS with an amazing and informative series of maps on city riots, including those that located people texting messages or those arrested. **Figure A.1** shows an overlay of the addresses of suspects in the rioting and poverty data.

Figure A.1

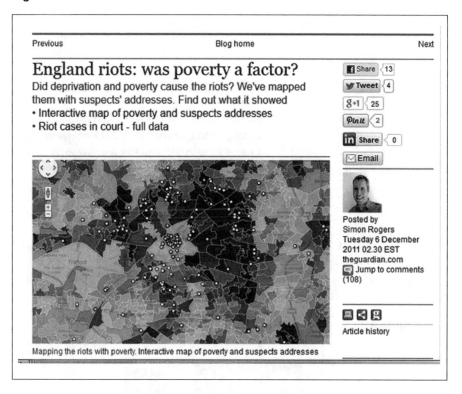

Mapping the riots with poverty. Interactive map of poverty and suspects addresses

Turning Matching Sideways

The major concept in mapping is the same one you encounter in database managers: matching. In Chapter 6, we discussed matching with the visual interface in Microsoft Access. With mapping software, the process is putting one layer of data on top of another, instead of drawing lines between fields. As is appropriate with mapping, let's illustrate how to do it.

In the first example, we will use a Google Fusion Table to look at a data set of local fires. The data set of building fires in the city of Champaign, Illinois, is fairly straightforward. After just a little data cleaning, we transformed it into date, time, and location columns for each fire from 2009 through 2013, as shown in **Figure A.2**.

Figure A.2

C2 ▼	f_x	1302 Hickory ST Champaign, IL	

	A	B	C
1	Alarm_Date	Alarm_Time	Address
2	1-Feb-09	14:29:03	1302 Hickory ST Champaign, IL
3	2-Feb-09	6:53:09	602 W Marketview DR Champaign, IL
4	15-Feb-09	20:13:33	1008 N Willis AVE Champaign, IL
5	17-Feb-09	21:48:00	902 E University AVE Champaign, IL
6	18-Feb-09	23:47:59	1703 W White ST Champaign, IL
7	28-Feb-09	18:42:31	409 Chalmers ST Champaign, IL
8	19-Mar-09	16:05:40	2003 W John ST Champaign, IL
9	24-Mar-09	20:26:16	401 E John ST Champaign, IL

To upload the spreadsheet into Google Fusion Tables, we will need to have registered a free Google Drive account, which is a filing space online. Once you have this account, all you have to do is click on "Drive," as shown in **Figure A.3**.

Figure A.3

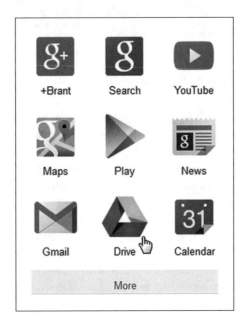

Next, click on "CREATE" and then choose "Fusion Table" in your options, as in **Figure A.4**.

Figure A.4

You will be taken to a screen that enables you to connect to a file—on your computer, on your Google Drive, or from a Website address—or to create an empty table. In this case, we browsed our computer folders for the spreadsheet named ChampaignFiresReports (see **Figure A.5**).

Figure A.5

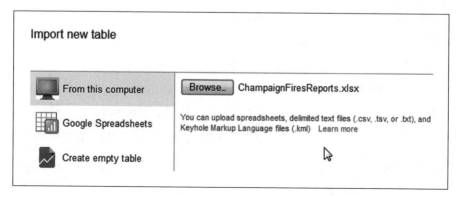

We click on "Next," and the program takes us to a screen that shows the spreadsheet. We click on "Next" again, as in **Figure A.6**.

Figure A.6

Import new table				✕
Column names are in row 1 ▾				
1	Alar...	Alar...	Address	
2	1-Feb-09	14:29:03	1302 Hickory ST Champaign, IL	
3	2-Feb-09	6:53:09	602 W Marketview DR Champaign, IL	
4	15-Feb-09	20:13:33	1008 N Willis AVE Champaign, IL	
5	17-Feb-09	21:48:00	902 E University AVE Champaign, IL	
6	18-Feb-09	23:47:59	1703 W White ST Champaign, IL	
7	28-Feb-09	18:42:31	409 Chalmers ST Champaign, IL	
8	19-Mar-09	16:05:40	2003 W John ST	

Rows before the header row will be ignored.

New to Fusion Tables?
Take a peek! Play with a data set or try a tutorial.   Cancel   « Back   Next »

The program now takes us to one last import screen, shown in **Figure A.7**. Here, you can add notes about the file. When you are done adding your notes, hit "Finish."

Figure A.7

Import new table	
Table name	ChampaignFiresReports
Allow export	☑ ⓘ
Attribute data to	ⓘ
Attribution page link	
Description	Imported at Sun Mar 23 17:47:49 PDT 2014 from ChampaignFiresReports.xlsx.
	For example, what would you like to remember about this table in a year?

New to Fusion Tables?
Take a peek! Play with a data set or try a tutorial.   Cancel   « Back   Finish

The file will import into Google Fusion Tables, initially showing up on the "Rows" tab where it looks like the spreadsheet, but with the location automatically highlighted. (The program will always choose the likeliest column to be the location; sometimes you will have to choose a different column or rearrange your data.) See **Figure A.8**.

Figure A.8

When you click on "Map of Address," the program will start *geocoding* the data, meaning it is matching the address with the template of geographical information—that is, with a map. (This process happens in some form with every kind of mapping software.) As you can see in **Figure A.9**, the program is also letting you know if any of the locations are ambiguous.

Figure A.9

When it is finished geocoding, the program will show you a map that you may have to zoom in on, using the tool by the cursor. The location of each fire in Champaign over the past five years is marked with a red dot on the map, allowing you to see patterns. If you want, you can click on one of the dots to get the information about that specific fire, as shown in **Figure A.10**.

Figure A.10

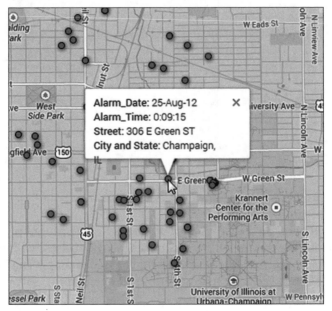

If you want to see a more general pattern, you can switch to "Heatmap." By clicking on the "Heatmap" button, you move from points to shading. The shading does not represent the heat of the fire but instead represents clusters of fires through intensity of shade or color (see **Figure A.11**).

Figure A.11

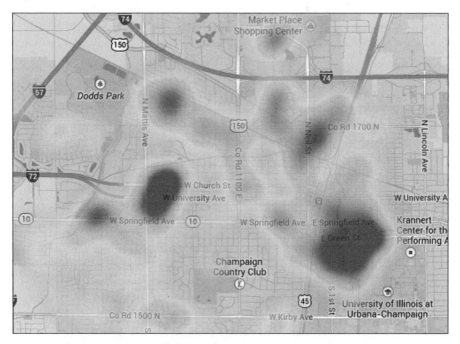

Maps Using Different Location Data

Longitude and latitude data are often more reliable than street addresses. In this example, we will use Esri Maps, which can be added to Microsoft Excel. The advantage of mapping with Esri software is that it has been used by many government agencies and hundreds of thousands of people for years, and there are many ready-made map layers for streets, rivers, terrain, and other geographical features.

In this case, we have data downloaded from the state of Illinois environmental Website. This data is about leaking underground storage tanks—usually old petroleum tanks polluting the nearby land and water with gasoline or other products. The data set is shown in **Figure A.12**.

Figure A.12

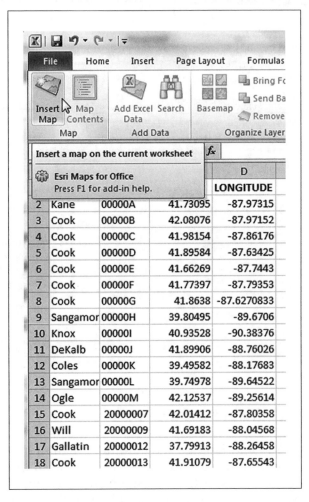

So long as you are signed in with a user account, you can click on "Insert Map" and go directly to a screen where you can upload the data. You create a map by adding layers of maps from your files—in this case, the leaking underground storage file in comma-separated values (CSV) format—or from existing base maps, as in **Figure A.13**.

Figure A.13

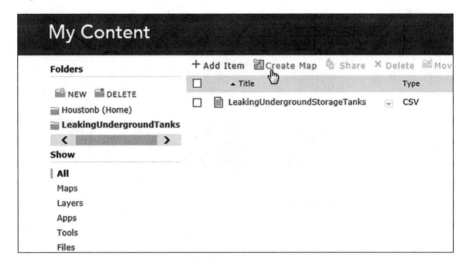

After clicking on "Create Map," you can upload your file by adding a layer and choosing the leaking tank data, as in **Figure A.14**.

Figure A.14

When you add your file through the usual import procedure, your dots identifying locations will be based on longitude and latitude. You then can add a base map of streets and highways, as in **Figure A.15**.

Figure A.15

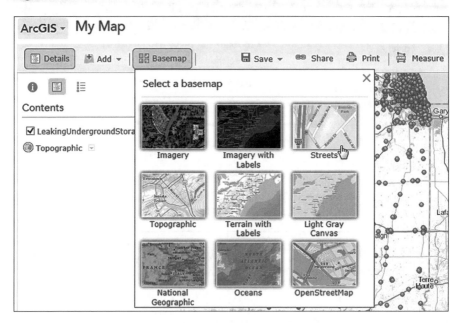

When you click on the base map called "Streets," you will see highways, streets, and even streams (see **Figure A.16**). This allows you to start analyzing clusters of leaking tanks and their proximity to water as the basis for your reporting.

Figure A.16

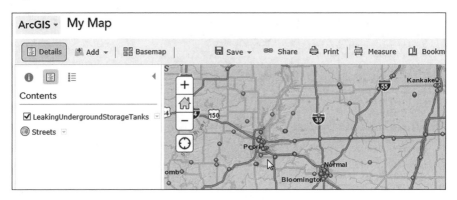

Appendix B

A Short Introduction to Social Network Analysis

Throughout this book, we have looked at the most basic approaches to data analyses currently being used by journalists for producing stories. There is another approach common to social sciences that journalists have begun to use more frequently: social network analysis. It is not surprising with the rise of social media, such as Facebook and Twitter, that this method of analysis of social structure would gain new popularity and interest.

The concepts of social network analysis began developing in the 1930s, but took a big leap ahead when computer graphics became available in the 1970s. One of the first uses of this technique happened in 1976 when journalists set out to investigate organized crime and public corruption in Phoenix, Arizona, after a car bomb killed investigative reporter Don Bolles. During the investigation, known as the Arizona Project, journalists worked with a University of Arizona professor to illustrate the power of an informal group of politicians and businessmen known as the Phoenix 40. The social network analysis provided the journalists with a social "road map" of the underpinnings of a corrupt system.

Social network analysis did not start to become an integral part of computer-assisted reporting (CAR) until the early years of the twenty-first century. In one example, two University of Missouri graduate students, Jaimi Dowdell and Aaron Kessler, worked with *The Kansas City Star* in 2004. Together, they revealed a network that the U.S. government believed connected a relief agency and an alleged operative in Columbia, Missouri, to terrorist Osama bin Laden.

In 2007, Ronald Campbell, then at *The Orange County Register* in California, used more than 10,000 pages of court records, financial reports, and other documents to expose a network created by an imprisoned charity telemarketer, Mitch Gold, to raise money for charities and "keep all but just 7 cents on the dollar for charity." Campbell worked with a multimedia staff member, Geoffrey Anderson, to include an interactive social network analysis tool on the Web, as shown in **Figure B.1**.

Figure B.1

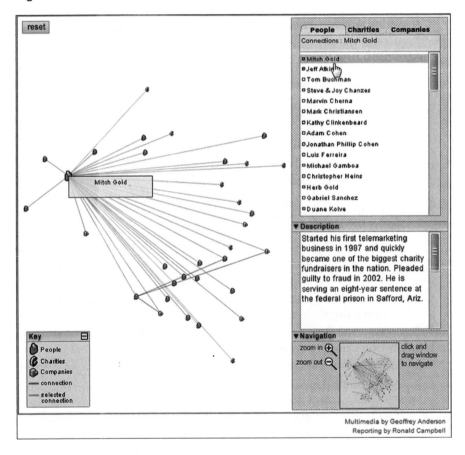

"The Mitch Gold story was like a big ball of spaghetti: It involved dozens of characters, many companies and nonprofits (some of them legitimate, some of them fraudulent), several states," Campbell recalled. "When I started, the only thing I knew was the person at the center: Mitch," Campbell said. "Social network analysis gave me a tool to link everything together and to understand which characters and companies were the most important and which ones were peripheral actors. That understanding in turn guided me when it came time to write the story."

More recently, the Organized Crime and Corruption Reporting Project used network analysis to follow international money laundering. In another example, a Korean investigative news agency used social network analysis to uncover about 600 Twitter accounts suspected to be related to an undercover government agency trying to influence elections.

In yet another example, *The Washington Post* used social network analysis to report on a group of language schools in the Los Angeles area that appeared to be "visa mills" for foreign students. Using a database of a student visas, the newspaper showed that a total of twenty-two related language schools in the Los Angeles area had accounted for 33,000 visas issued—many good for up to two years.

Visualizing Relationships

Many other professions have been using social network analysis for some time. Among the users are business consultants, intelligence and law enforcement agencies, public health investigators, sociologists, and anthropologists.

Using free or inexpensive computer software such as NodeXL, Gephi, UCINET, or Pajek, researchers look at social structures. The software and mathematical analysis basically allows the researcher to map relationships and the strength and the placement of those relationships in the social structure being analyzed.

As Ken Frank, who has taught the topic at Michigan State University, commented, "Network analysis is based on the intuitive notion that these patterns are important features of the lives of the individuals who display them. Network analysts believe that how an individual lives depends in large part on how that individual is tied into the larger web of social connections."

Quite often the data used for this approach is survey data. For example, public health researchers in Hartford, Connecticut, tracked and mapped the relationships between individuals who purchased heroin, those they purchased it from, users who injected it together, and how race affected use. The researchers gathered the data by surveying heroin users; the survey results were the data set used in the network analysis.

Journalists and the public became more aware of this kind of analysis following the 2001 terrorist attacks against the World Trade Center and the Pentagon. A practitioner of this method, business consultant Valdis E. Krebs, quickly outlined the possible relationships and organization of the nineteen terrorists involved in the attack. Using open sources—that is, information from newspapers—Krebs was able to visually portray the terrorists' contacts. Krebs published an article, "Mapping Networks of Terrorist Cells," in the magazine *Connections* with his own computer-produced maps of relationships, as shown in **Figure B.2.**

Figure B.2

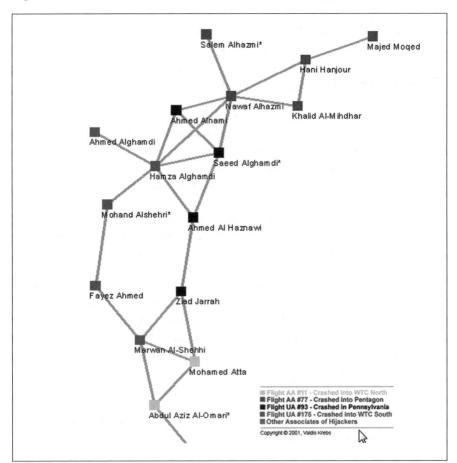

Accompanying this diagram and others were color codes for each of the terrorists that noted which airline crash they were involved with. The diagrams showed which terrorists had met with which other terrorists according to records in the public purview—newspapers clips and leaks from law enforcement. The diagram showed who belonged to which terrorist cell and the frequency of contacts between members. It also showed how isolated each cell could be to ensure secrecy. This is a dramatic example of the use of social network analysis, but it shows the power to visualize relationships, especially in large data sets.

A Different Way to Look at Data

Like the other computer-assisted techniques you have learned, social network analysis has its own language and that language can vary by software. Essentially, all software uses dots to represent persons or institutions and lines to represent the connections. In some software, these elements are called *nodes* and *ties*, or *vertices* and *edges*.

Social network analysis also looks at information differently than the traditional format of columns and rows. In a regular worksheet, each column is a category of information and each row is a record. But in some social network software, a matrix is created in which every person and institution is listed in every row and every column. When they are connected, a cell is marked 1; when they are not connected, the cell is marked 0.

A more recent version of free social network analysis software, NodeXL, is an add-on to Microsoft Excel and makes data entry a bit simpler. After opening a NodeXL worksheet, we entered the fictional names of corporate executives who sit on various boards of directors and the names of the companies on whose boards they sit. As shown in **Figure B.3**, their names are in Vertex 1, and the board they sit on is Vertex 2.

Note the insert box in **Figure B.3**, where it shows we are entering data in the "Edges" tab.

Figure B.3

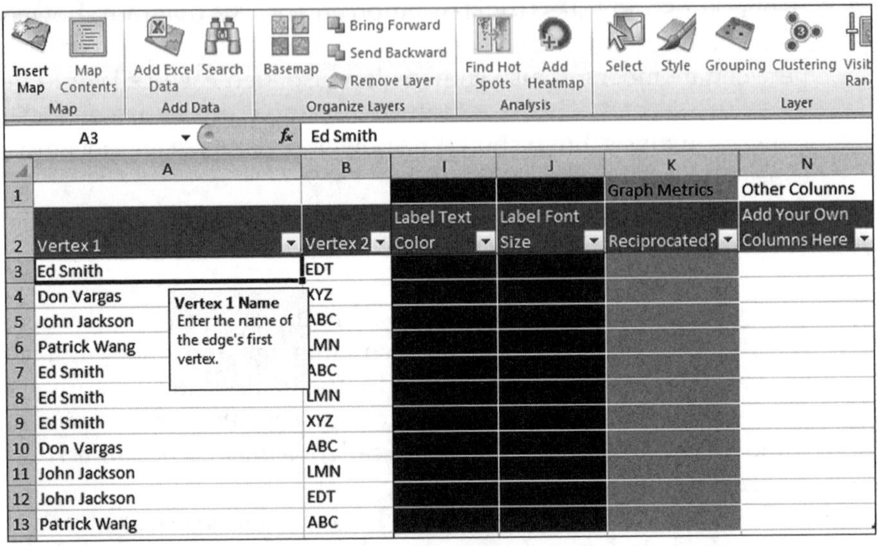

If we move to the Vertices tab, which is at the bottom of the screen, we see the program allows us to label the Vertices with names, as displayed in **Figure B.4**, so that they will show up on our eventual diagram.

Figure B.4

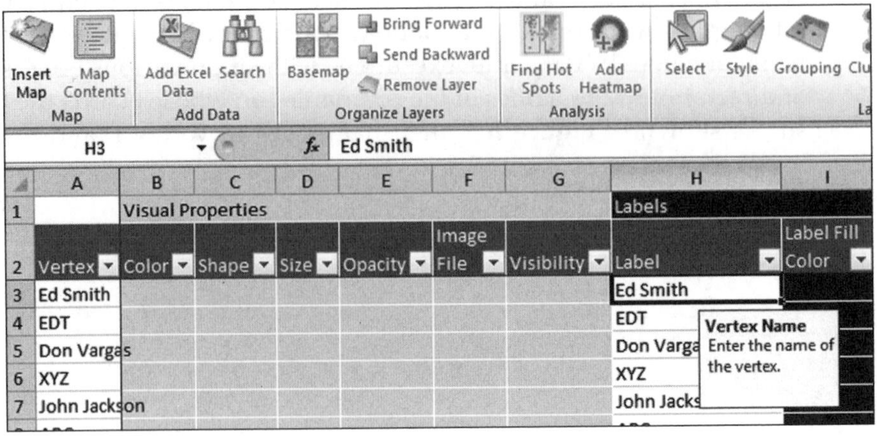

Once we have all our names entered, we transform them into a graph or diagram. There are several steps involved, but you can see the rudimentary diagram we can produce without too much work in **Figure B.5**. As you can easily see in this small data set, some of these executives sit on the board of each other's companies, with Ed Smith sitting on the most boards.

Figure B.5

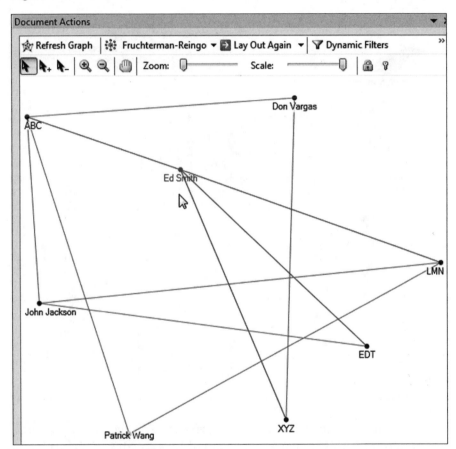

In recent years, business reporters have delved into questions raised by interlocking directorships on boards and potential conflicts of interest. One famous project was "TheyRule," which looked at 100 corporate boards with an easy-to-use interactive tool (see **Figure B.6**).

Figure B.6

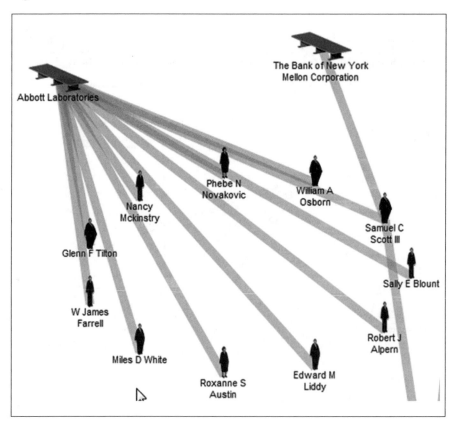

Another Website created by journalists and technologists to do ongoing social network analysis is Muckety.com, which offers a diagram of itself on its About page, as in **Figure B.7**.

Figure B.7

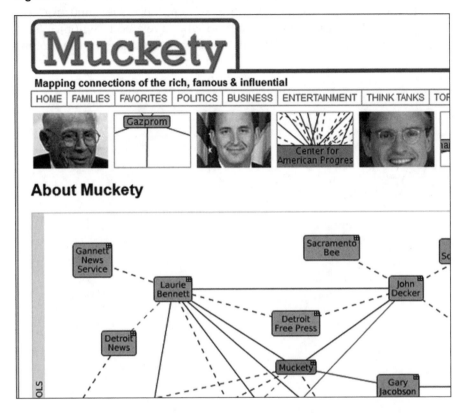

Depending on the data set and the analysis, social network analysis maps can go far beyond the diagrams shown so far. Experts use mathematical techniques to determine the importance of a person or entity in a network as well as to measure the distance and closeness of relationships. This allows you to see how many degrees of separation there are.

Even basic use of this analysis can be helpful in understanding how decisions and policies are made. It shows how people interact and what patterns evolve through these interactions, which is what journalists observe and write about every day. Again, it requires more than seeing connections. It involves interviews and understanding the strength of a connection and its real influence.

By applying these techniques to your community, you could start to more closely track who knows whom, who is isolated from the powerful and disenfranchised, and who is related to whom. With a better understanding of the relationships, you can ask more probing questions or better prepare for a routine interview.

Appendix C

Choosing Hardware and Software

As longtime computer-assisted reporting (CAR) expert and teacher David Donald said, "I think working only online is still too limiting for CAR, even for beginners." However, choosing the right hardware and software for CAR can be difficult. There is an excess of information available about the various offerings and improvements to both hardware and software packages arrive monthly, if not weekly.

Those living in the world of computer science and programming and coding will suggest "open-source" and free software. But if you don't have their skills, you may find using such software frustrating. So, if you can use commercial software—because you can afford it or can get it free at a university—then use it.

In any case, you need to answer the following questions:

- What software do I need to perform my work and analysis?
- What kind of hardware do I need to run the software? How much random access memory (RAM) and how many gigabytes on the computer's hard drive do I need?
- What can I do online before considering how to proceed on my own computer?

At a minimum, you will need spreadsheet software and database manager software. The storage and memory requirements of the software will guide you in your selection of hardware. If you are going to do statistical analysis or data mapping, you need the most hard drive space and RAM you can get. In 2014, Donald suggested that you get as much RAM as possible for data analysis—16 gigabytes—and as spacious a hard drive as possible—even consider a terabyte.

As another longtime CAR practitioner and teacher, Jennifer LaFleur, said, "I wouldn't specify a number—I always say get as much as you can for your budget. Typically, desktops will be less expensive, but most folks want laptops these days."

You should also find out what kind of software your colleagues—in your newsroom or in the profession—use. You may want to choose their preferred brands, because if they are familiar with that software, they can help you learn it or discuss problems you encounter.

Journalists frequently use the following spreadsheets: Microsoft Excel or Excel Online or Google Spreadsheet. They frequently use the following database managers: Microsoft Access, MySQL, or Navicat.

In statistical software, the two most popular are SPSS and SAS. But such packages can be expensive outside a university; there is also statistical software known as R available at www.r-project.org. But many journalists are finding they can do most of their statistical work using Microsoft Excel or add-ons.

Journalists use mapping software such as Google Maps and Google Fusion Tables or Tableau. However, Esri products offer a great deal of data, plus Esri has made more of its software and data free.

To keep up with hardware and software changes, prices, and quality, read commercial computer magazines or any other publications on the magazine stand and online that look helpful. For additional and more specific tips, subscribe to the National Institute for Computer-Assisted Reporting listserv, nicar-l (accessed through www.ire.org/nicar/).

Selected Bibliography

Books and Articles

Cairo, Albert. *The Functional Art: An Introduction to Information Graphics and Visualization.* Berkeley, CA: New Riders, 2013.

Cohen, Sarah. *Numbers in the Newsroom: Using Math and Statistics in News.* Columbia, MO: Investigative Reporters and Editors, 2014.

Cuillier, David, and Charles N. Davis. *The Art of Access: Strategies for Acquiring Public Records.* Washington, DC: CQ, 2011.

Egawhary, Elena, and Cynthia O'Murchu. *Data Journalism* (handbook). The Centre for Investigative Journalism. http://tcij.org/resources/handbooks/data-journalism.

Foust, James C. *Online Journalism: Principles and Practices for News on the Web.* 3rd ed. Scottsdale, AZ: Holcomb Hathaway, 2011.

Gray, Jonathan, Liliana Bounegru, and Lucy Chamber, eds. *The Data Journalism Handbook: How Journalists Can Use Data to Improve the News.* Sebastopol, CA: O'Reilly Media, 2012. http://datajournalismhandbook.org/1.0/en/.

Houston, Brant, and Investigative Reporters and Editors, eds. *The Investigative Reporter's Handbook: A Guide to Documents, Databases, and Techniques.* 5th ed. Boston: Bedford/St. Martin's, 2009.

Huff, Darrell. *How to Lie with Statistics.* New York: W.W. Norton, 1993.

Ingram, Matthew. "The Golden Age of Computer-Assisted Reporting Is At Hand," *Nieman Journalism Lab*, May 20, 2009. www.niemanlab.org/2009/05/the-golden-age-of-computer-assisted-reporting-is-at-hand/.

Jones, Gerald Everett. *How to Lie with Charts.* 2nd ed. Santa Monica, CA: LaPuerta, 2007.

Meyer, Philip. *Precision Journalism: A Reporter's Introduction to Social Science Methods*. 4th ed. Lanham, MD: Rowman & Littlefield, 2002.

Method, Jason. "The Benefits of Computer-Assisted Reporting," *Nieman Reports*, Fall 2008. http://nieman.harvard.edu/reports/article/100454/The-Benefits-of-Computer-Assisted-Reporting.aspx.

Monmonier, Mark. *How to Lie with Maps*. 2nd ed. Chicago: University of Chicago Press, 1996.

Paulos, John Allen. *Beyond Numeracy: Ruminations of a Numbers Man*. New York: Vintage, 1992.

Tufte, Edward R. *Envisioning Information*. Cheshire, CT: Graphics, 1990.

Vallance-Jones, Fred, and David McKie; with Aron Pilhofer and Jaimi Dowdell. *Computer-Assisted Reporting: A Comprehensive Primer.* Don Mills, Ontario; New York: Oxford University Press, 2009.

Winkleman, Simon, ed. *Data Journalism in Asia: A collection of Articles from Members of the Society of Asian Journalists (AJ)*. Singapore: Konrad-Adenauer-Stiftung, 2013. www.kas.de/wf/doc/kas_35547-1522-2-30.pdf?130930105417.

Websites

African News Innovation Challenge. http://africannewschallenge.org.

Association of Public Data Users. http://apdu.org.

Center for Investigative Reporting. http://cironline.org.

Center for Investigative Reporting, Jennifer LaFleur's blog. http://cironline.org/person/jennifer-lafleur.

Center for Responsive Politics. www.opensecrets.org.

Centre for Investigative Journalism. http://tcij.org.

Columbia Journalism Review, Data Points, Exploring Data Journalism. www.cjr.org/data_points/.

Data Driven Journalism, Where Journalism Meets Data. http://datadrivenjournalism.net.

Data Journalism Blog. www.datajournalismblog.com.

Data Journalism Blog, Paul Bradshaw's blog. www.datajournalismblog.com/tag/paul-bradshaw/.

Data.gov. www.data.gov.

Global Investigative Journalism Network, Data Journalism. http://gijn.org/resources/data-journalism/.

The Guardian, Data Journalism. www.theguardian.com/media/data-journalism.

Guidestar. www.guidestar.org.

International Consortium of Investigative Journalists, Computer-Assisted Repo
ing. www.icij.org/tags/computer-assisted-reporting.

Investigative Reporters and Editors. www.ire.org.

Investigative Reporters and Editors, Resource Center. www.ire.org/resource-
center/.

LexisNexis. www.lexisnexis.com.

Muckety, Mapping connections of the rich, famous, and influential. http://muckety.
com.

National Institute for Computer-Assisted Reporting. www.ire.org/nicar/.

National Institute on Money in State Politics. www.followthemoney.org.

NewsBank. www.newsbank.com.

ProPublica, Journalism in the Public Interest. www.propublica.org.

Pulitzer Prizes. www.pulitzer.org.

R, The R Project for Statistical Computing. www.r-project.org.

Reporters Committee for Freedom of the Press. www.rcfp.org.

Research Clinic, Investigative Research Links and Articles by Paul Myers. http://
researchclinic.net.

SearchSystems.net, Free Public Records. www.searchsystems.net.

UNdata. http://data.un.org.

United Network for Organ Sharing. www.unos.org.

U.S. Bureau of Alcohol, Tobacco, Firearms and Explosives. www.atf.gov.

U.S. Census Bureau. www.census.gov.

U.S. Government Accountability Office. www.gao.gov.

U.S. Small Business Administration, www.sba.gov.

Sources for Key Examples

The examples at the beginning of the chapters and in CAR Wars were selected
from *Uplink*, the newsletter and blog on computer-assisted reporting created and
maintained by Investigative Reporters and Editors and the National Institute for
Computer-Assisted Reporting at www.ire.org/blog/uplink/.

Glossary

Address: In a spreadsheet, the location, or cell, on a worksheet identified by a letter and number.

American Standard Code for Information Interchange (ASCII): Almost always referred to by the acronym, which is pronounced "ask-key," this is the most simple and common file format. A file in this format looks like a text file and can be read by most software programs.

Ascending: Sorting items in order of low to high value.

Average: This usually refers to the total amount divided by the number of items making up the amount. In math and statistics, this amount is called mean; in math, average also refers to median or mode. *See also* Median; Mode

Boolean logic: A way of searching online and in database managers using the words *and*, *or*, and *not* to filter information.

Browser: Software, such as Firefox, Internet Explorer, or Safari, that allows you to view and read pages on the World Wide Web.

Byte: A measure of the amount of data storage that is composed of eight bits.

Cells: In a spreadsheet, a box containing information. *See also* Address

Cloud: A remote server that can provide not only storage on the Internet, but also software, computing, and other services.

Codebook: A document, also sometimes called a code sheet or data dictionary, used for deciphering codes in a database.

Columns: A vertical set of cells storing information in a worksheet. *See also* Cells; Rows; Worksheet

Comma-separated values (CSV): This data format separates columns by commas or other punctuation. This commonly used format compacts a data set, but it is easily opened by spreadsheets and other software.

Computer-assisted reporting (CAR): Finding, processing, and analyzing data as part of the reporting work in journalism.

Database: A file or collection of related data files, sometimes known as tables.

Database manager: A software program organizing and analyzing information in a database. Database managers used by journalists include Microsoft Access, MySQL, and Navicat.

Descending: Sorting items in order of high to low value.

Digital news services: Commercial collections of news articles, court cases, and other information that can be valuable in finding useful data. Examples include LexisNexis and NewsBank.

Dirty data: Data incorrectly entered into a data set through typos or miscoding. *See also* String function

Downloading: Transferring files from another computer or from an online source to your own computer or storage media.

Enterprise matchmaking: Joining databases that have not been set up to be joined, enabling comparison of the data.

Field: A specific set of information, such as a column in a spreadsheet. *See also* Key fields

File transfer protocol (FTP): A program language that permits the user to transfer a file from one computer to another.

Filter: To selectively extract a subset of data from a larger data set.

From statement: An SQL statement that identifies the database or table to be looked at. *See also* Structured Query Language (SQL)

Geographic information system (GIS): *See* Mapping software

Google Groups: A group of people interested in the same topic who receive and send e-mails to others in the group.

Group By statement: An SQL statement that divides records into groups based on identical fields. *See also* Grouping; Pivot table; Structured Query Language (SQL)

Grouping: Dividing similar data into groups. *See also* Group By statement

Having statement: A statement that selects records by selected criteria after they have been grouped. Acts like a Where statement does on individual records in SQL. *See also* Select statement; Structured Query Language (SQL); Where statement

Hits: *See* Matches/hits

Hypertext: In text files, highlighted words, known as links. Clicking on a link transfers you to another file or page on the Web.

Hypertext Markup Language (HTML): The standard markup language used to create Web pages.

Key fields: The fields (columns) in a database manager that are used to properly join records in one table with one or more other tables.

Listserv: A discussion group on the Internet about a particular topic. Messages sent to the listserv go to all those who have joined, arriving in individual emails or in a list (digest form).

Mapping software: Specialized software, also known as a geographic information system (GIS), that produces maps by matching templates such as street addresses to data files imported into the software. Examples include Esri, Google Maps, and Google Fusion Tables or Tableau.

Matches/hits: Finding identical information in the key fields of two or more files, or tables, in a relational database. *See also* Key fields; Relational database

Mean: *See* Average.

Median: An average that is the middle value in a series of numbers. Half of the numbers are higher and half are lower than the median.

Mode: An average that is the number most often occurring in a series of numbers. For example, the most frequent (not majority) salary in a group of people would be the mode.

Observation: A record in statistical software.

Order by statement: An SQL statement that sorts records based on one or more fields. *See also* Structured Query Language (SQL)

Outlier: Number at the extreme of a series of numbers.

Parsing: Dividing a column into two or more columns.

Percentage: The proportion of one number to another.

Percentage difference: The proportion of change between two sets of numbers.

Pivot table: A table of information that allows you to total numbers in different groups and to count or sum the total in each group. It works similarly to Group By in database managers. *See also* Database manager; Group By statement

Portable Document Format (PDF): This file format stores data in a rigid way that must be converted to a spreadsheet or other format before the data can be processed and analyzed.

Query: A way to select, filter, group, and sort information in a database using a database manager. *See also* Database manager; Structured Query Language (SQL)

Rates: The number of occurrences divided by the population in which the occurrences happen, such as twelve murders per 100,000 persons.

Ratio: One number divided by another to give a sense of proportion, such as three to one.

Record: In a database manager, a row of information across fields (columns).

Record layout: Information about the names and size of fields in a database.

Relational database: A database composed of tables that can be joined through key fields. *See also* Key fields

Rows: A horizontal set of cells storing information in a worksheet. *See also* Cells; Columns; Worksheet

Search tool: A program that allows you to search for information on the Internet.

Searchers: Experts who know how to find information on the Internet.

Select statement: A statement in SQL that selects the fields (or columns) to look at. *See also* Having statement; Structured Query Language (SQL); Where statement

Sort: The process of reordering data in a column based on its value. *See also* Ascending; Descending

Spreadsheet: Part of a software program used for calculations, budgets, and other number-related tasks and/or to filter or organize data sets. Organized in a grid pattern by rows and columns, a spreadsheet may contain multiple worksheets. Programs used by journalists include Microsoft Excel or Excel Online and Google Spreadsheet. *See also* Worksheet

Statistical software: Packages used for analyzing statistical data. Popular programs include SAS (Statistical Analysis System), SPSS (Statistical Software for the Political and Social Sciences), and R.

String function: Programming that cleans up dirty data by standardizing a series of letters or numbers.

Structured Query Language (SQL): This language is used for querying a database to do calculations and reorganize or recode data, as well as to join tables.

Summary data: Data that has been divided into groups and totaled, providing a summary of the data set.

Tables: A table is a file in a database manager—just as a worksheet is a file in a spreadsheet. It consists of fields (columns) and records (rows).

Tabular: Information presented in a table of columns and rows.

Uniform Resource Locator (URL): The address of a Website on the Internet.

Web scraping: In journalism, the use of a program to automatically download data from the Web into a database, particularly when the records can only be viewed one at a time or in small groups.

Where statement: A statement in SQL that selects by criteria the records to look at within a database. *See also* Having statement; Select statement; Structured Query Language (SQL)

Worksheet: A file of columns and rows of information within a spreadsheet. *See also* Columns; Rows; Spreadsheet

Zip: To compress one or more files so that information can be stored and transferred more efficiently.

Index

I

About the Author

Brant Houston is a professor and the Knight Chair in Investigative Reporting at the University of Illinois, where he teaches journalism and oversees an online newsroom. An award-winning journalist, he was an investigative reporter at U.S. newspapers for seventeen years. For more than a decade, he served as the executive director of Investigative Reporters and Editors, a 5,000-member association headquartered at the University of Missouri School of Journalism, where he also taught investigative reporting. Houston has conducted over 300 seminars for professional journalists and students in twenty-five countries, and he is a co-founder of international networks serving educators and connecting nonprofit newsrooms.